SPEAKING OF
CHAUCER

SPEAKING OF CHAUCER

BY

E. TALBOT DONALDSON

W · W · NORTON & COMPANY · INC ·

NEW YORK

84979

For
DEIRDRE

PREFACE

THE WRITER of a preface to a collection such as this, two-thirds of whose essays have appeared in print before, would be hard put to it to devise a modesty formula capable of concealing his vanity; all he can do is hope that some readers will derive enough pleasure from the collection to be willing to overlook the offence. All but the shortest of these pieces were originally written as lectures that I admit I enjoyed delivering, and I do not think I should have done so if I had not felt that my audiences were in general pleased. In any case, I should be most happy if in book form these essays might receive so courteous a reception as they did when they were first presented.

I had initially planned to revise some of those that have been printed before in order to clarify points that it seemed to me certain of my readers had misunderstood. But I found that my revisions succeeded in saying exactly what I had said before, only more long-windedly; and when I closely examined the criticism of those scholars who I thought had misunderstood what I had written, I discovered, ruefully enough, that they had understood it perfectly well—they had merely disapproved of it. Therefore I limited my revision to the correction of errors and to the elimination from several of the previously printed pieces of material which, while only of ancillary value in its original context, became the principal subject of essays written later. It would perhaps have been more scholarly of me to append to several of the controversial articles—notably 'Chaucer the Pilgrim' and 'The Ending of Troilus'—a bibliography of dissent, but this task has been made less necessary by the contributions of Dieter Mehl and Hans Käsmann to the recent *Festschrift* for Professor Walter F. Schirmer.[1] I ought to say that I am

---

[1] *Chaucer und seine Zeit*, ed. Arno Esch (Tübingen, 1968). In his essay, 'Erscheinungsformen des Erzählers in Chaucers "Canterbury Tales"', Professor

greatly impressed by both the quality and the quantity of contrary opinion—impressed but not persuaded.

Among the many things that I am grateful for in my professional life is the series of events—wholly unforeseen by me—that first made me a teacher of Chaucer, which is surely one of the pleasantest occupations open to an academic. For the fact is that Chaucer often teaches himself, so that one is apt to find oneself in the classroom not at the lectern explicating the text but sitting with one's students as part of a delighted audience before whom the text unfolds itself. And to the enthusiastic and articulate response of my students, both at Yale and at Columbia, I owe a great deal for my own understanding of Chaucer's works. I am also, of course, greatly indebted to many fellow Chaucerians, both of this and of earlier generations: in rereading the literature of the field I am struck with mingled horror and gratitude as I come upon the words which I had forgotten first impelled me towards my most prized ideas: 'Ther nis no newe gise that it nas old.' This indebtedness, I should add, extends to those with whom I am in large disagreement and whom, in the heat of argument, I may have treated less than graciously. To two scholars I am privileged to number among my friends I owe a special debt: George Kane, whose great knowledge and logical powers have both supplied me with tools and kept them sharp; and John Pope, a Pierian spring of learning and imagination, from many a long lunch with whom I have come away with ideas that I have shamelessly developed into my own. Indeed, I do not see how I could have been more fortunate in my poet, my students, and my colleagues.

The previously printed essays first appeared in the following books and journals, whose editors and publishers I wish to thank for their permission to republish: 'Chaucer the Pilgrim', *Publications of the Modern Language Association of America*, lxix (1954); 'Idiom of Popular Poetry in the Miller's Tale', *English Institute Essays 1950*, ed. A. S. Downer (New York: Columbia University Press, 1951): reprinted in *Explication as Criticism*:

Mehl mentions, I believe, all the relevant discussions of the pilgrim Chaucer, and Professor Käsmann does the same for the ending of *Troilus* in his essay ' "I wolde excuse hire yit for routhe." Chaucers Einstellung zu Criseyde'.

Selected Papers from the English Institute 1941–1952, ed. W. K. Wimsatt, Jr (New York: Columbia University Press, 1963); 'The Ending of Chaucer's *Troilus*', *Early English and Norse Studies Presented to Hugh Smith,* ed. Arthur Brown and Peter Foote (London: Methuen, 1963); 'The Psychology of Editors of Middle English Texts', *English Studies Today 4,* ed. I. Cellini and G. Melchiori (Rome: Edizioni di Storia e Letteratura, 1966); '*Canterbury Tales,* D117: A Critical Edition', *Speculum,* xl (1965); 'Miller's Tale, A3483–6', *Modern Language Notes,* lxix (1954); 'Patristic Exegesis in the Criticism of Medieval Literature: The Opposition', *Critical Approaches to Medieval Literature: Selected Papers from the English Institute, 1958–1959,* ed. Dorothy Bethurum (New York: Columbia University Press, 1960); 'The Myth of Courtly Love', *Ventures: Magazine of the Yale Graduate School,* v (1965).

New York,   E. TALBOT DONALDSON
23 May 1969

CONTENTS

NOTE

IN QUOTING from Chaucer I have used, for passages where it is available, my edition of selections, *Chaucer's Poetry: An Anthology for the Modern Reader* (New York: The Ronald Press, 1958), though the line numbering I give here is uniformly that of the standard complete editions. The chief of these is, of course, that of F. N. Robinson, *The Works of Geoffrey Chaucer*, 2nd ed. (Boston, Mass: Houghton Mifflin Co., 1957), which I refer to as Robinson and have used for quotations from Chaucer's works omitted from my anthology. Frequent reference is also made to J. M. Manly and Edith Rickert, *The Text of the Canterbury Tales*, 8 vols. (Chicago: University of Chicago Press, 1940), cited as M-R; and to J. S. P. Tatlock and Arthur G. Kennedy, *A Concordance to the Complete Works of Geoffrey Chaucer* (Washington: Carnegie Institution, 1927), cited as *Concordance*.

1

CHAUCER THE PILGRIM

VERISIMILITUDE in a work of fiction is not without its attendant dangers, the chief of which is that the responses it stimulates in the reader may be those appropriate not so much to an imaginative production as to an historical one or to a piece of reporting. History and reporting are, of course, honourable in themselves, but if we react to a poet as though he were an historian or a reporter, we do him somewhat less than justice. I am under the impression that many readers, too much influenced by Chaucer's brilliant verisimilitude, tend to regard his famous pilgrimage to Canterbury as significant not because it is a great fiction, but because it seems to be a remarkable record of a fourteenth-century pilgrimage. A remarkable record it may be, but if we treat it too narrowly as such there are going to be certain casualties among the elements that make up the fiction. Perhaps first among these elements is the fictional reporter, Chaucer the pilgrim, and the role he plays in the Prologue to the *Canterbury Tales* and in the links between them. I think it time that he was rescued from the comparatively dull record of history and put back into his poem. He is not really Chaucer the poet—nor, for that matter, is either the poet, or the poem's protagonist, that Geoffrey Chaucer frequently mentioned in contemporary historical records as a distinguished civil servant, but never as a poet. The fact that these are three separate entities does not, naturally, exclude the probability—or rather the certainty—that they bore a close resemblance to one another, and that, indeed, they frequently got together in the same body. But that does not excuse us from keeping them distinct from one another, difficult as their close resemblance makes our task.

The natural tendency to confuse one thing with its like is perhaps best represented by a school of Chaucerian criticism, now outmoded, that pictured a single Chaucer under the guise of a wide-eyed, jolly, rolypoly little man who, on fine Spring mornings, used to get up early, while the dew was still on the grass, and go look at daisies. A charming portrait, this, so charming, indeed, that it was sometimes able to maintain itself to the exclusion of any Chaucerian other side. It has every reason to be charming, since it was lifted almost *in toto* from the version Chaucer gives of himself in the Prologue to the *Legend of Good Women*, though I imagine it owes some of its popularity to a rough analogy with Wordsworth—a sort of *Legend of Good Poets*. It was this version of Chaucer that Kittredge, in a page of great importance to Chaucer criticism, demolished with his assertion that 'a naïf Collector of Customs would be a paradoxical monster'. He might well have added that a naïve creator of old January would be even more monstrous.

Kittredge's pronouncement cleared the air, and most of us now accept the proposition that Chaucer was sophisticated as readily as we do the proposition that the whale is a mammal. But unhappily, now that we've got rid of the naïve fiction, it is easy to fall into the opposite sort of mistake. This is to envision, in the *Canterbury Tales*, a highly urbane, literal-historical Chaucer setting out from Southwark on a specific day of a specific year (we even argue somewhat acrimoniously about dates and routes), in company with a group of persons who existed in real life and whom Chaucer, his reporter's eye peeled for every idiosyncrasy, determined to get down on paper—down, that is, to the last wart—so that books might be written identifying them. Whenever this accurate reporter says something especially fatuous—which is not infrequently—it is either ascribed to an opinion peculiar to the Middle Ages (sometimes very peculiar), or else Chaucer's tongue is said to be in his cheek.

Now a Chaucer with tongue-in-cheek is a vast improvement over a simple-minded Chaucer when one is trying to define the whole man, but it must lead to a loss of critical perception, and in particular to a confused notion of Chaucerian irony, to see in the Prologue a reporter who is acutely aware of the significance of what he sees but who sometimes, for ironic emphasis, interprets the evidence presented by his observation in a fashion directly contrary to what we expect. The proposition ought to be expressed in reverse: the reporter is, usually, acutely unaware of the significance of what he sees, no matter how sharply he sees it. He is, to be sure, permitted his lucid intervals, but in general he is the victim of the poet's pervasive —not merely sporadic—irony. And as such he is also the chief agent by which the poet achieves his wonderfully complex, ironic, comic, serious vision of a world which is but a devious and confused, infinitely various pilgrimage to a certain shrine. It is, as I hope to make clear, a good deal more than merely fitting that our guide on such a pilgrimage should be a man of such naïveté as the Chaucer who tells the tale of *Sir Thopas*. Let us accompany him a little distance.

It is often remarked that Chaucer really liked the Prioress very much, even though he satirized her gently—very gently. But this is an understatement: Chaucer the pilgrim may not be said merely to have liked the Prioress very much—he thought she was utterly charming. In the first twenty-odd lines of her portrait (A118 ff.) he employs, among other superlatives, the adverb *ful* seven times. Middle English uses *ful* where we use *very*, and if one translates the beginning of the portrait into a kind of basic English (which is what, in a way, it really is), one gets something like this: 'There was also a Nun, a Prioress, who was very sincere and modest in the way she smiled; her biggest oath was only "By saint Loy"; and she was called Madame Eglantine. She sang the divine service very well, intoning it in her nose very prettily, and she spoke French very nicely and elegantly'—and so on, down to the last gasp of sentimental appreciation. Indeed, the Prioress may be said to have transformed the rhetoric into something not unlike that of a very bright kindergarten child's descriptive theme. In his reaction to the Prioress Chaucer the pilgrim resembles another—if less—simple-hearted enthusiast: the Host, whose summons to her to tell a tale must be one of the politest speeches in the language. Not 'My lady Prioresse, a tale now!' but, 'as curteisly as it hadde been a maide',

> My lady Prioresse, by youre leve,
> So that I wiste I sholde you nat greve,
> I wolde deemen that ye telle sholde

A tale next, if so were that ye wolde.
Now wol ye vouche sauf, my lady dere? (B²1636-41)

Where the Prioress reduced Chaucer to superlatives, she reduces the Host to subjunctives.

There is no need here to go deeply into the Prioress. Eileen Power's illustrations from contemporary episcopal records show with what extraordinary economy the portrait has been packed with abuses typical of fourteenth-century nuns. The abuses, to be sure, are mostly petty, but it is clear enough that the Prioress, while a perfect lady, is anything but a perfect nun; and attempts to whitewash her, of which there have been many, can only proceed from an innocence of heart equal to Chaucer the pilgrim's and undoubtedly directly influenced by it. For he, of course, is quite swept away by her irrelevant *sensibilité*, and as a result misses much of the point of what he sees. No doubt he feels that he has come a long way, socially speaking, since his encounter with the Black Knight in the forest, and he knows, or thinks he knows, a little more of what it's all about: in this case it seems to be mostly about good manners, kindness to animals, and female charm. Thus it has been argued that Chaucer's appreciation for the Prioress as a sort of heroine of courtly romance *manquée* actually reflects the sophistication of the living Chaucer, an urbane man who cared little whether amiable nuns were good nuns. But it seems a curious form of sophistication that permits itself to babble superlatives; and indeed, if this is sophistication, it is the kind generally seen in the least experienced people—one that reflects a wide-eyed wonder at the glamour of the great world. It is just what one might expect of a bourgeois exposed to the splendours of high society, whose values, such as they are, he eagerly accepts. And that is precisely what Chaucer the pilgrim is, and what he does.

If the Prioress's appeal to him is through elegant femininity, the Monk's is through imposing virility. Of this formidable and important prelate the pilgrim does not say, with Placebo,

I woot wel that my lord can more than I:
What that he saith, I holde it ferm and stable, (E1498-9)

but he acts Placebo's part to perfection. He is as impressed with the Monk as the Monk is, and accepts him on his own terms and at

face value, never sensing that those terms imply complete condemnation of Monk *qua* Monk. The Host is also impressed by
the Monk's virility, but having no sense of Placebonian propriety
(he is himself a most virile man) he makes indecent jokes about
it. This, naturally, offends the pilgrim's sense of decorum: there
is a note of deferential commiseration in his comment, 'This
worthy Monk took al in pacience' (B3155). Inevitably when the
Monk establishes hunting as the highest activity of which religious man is capable, 'I saide his opinion was good' (A183). As
one of the pilgrim's spiritual heirs was later to say, Very like a
whale; but not, of course, like a fish out of water.

Wholehearted approval for the values that important persons
subscribe to is seen again in the portrait of the Friar. This
amounts to a prolonged gratulation for the efficiency the de-
plorable Hubert shows in undermining the fabric of the Church
by turning St Francis's ideal inside out:

> Ful swetely herde he confessioun
> And plesant was his absolucioun.

> For unto swich a worthy man as he
> Accorded nat, as by his facultee,
> To have with sike lazars aquaintaunce. (A221-2, 243-5)

It is sometimes said that Chaucer did not like the Friar. Whether
Chaucer the man would have liked such a Friar is, for our present
purposes, irrelevant. But if the pilgrim does not unequivocally
express his liking for him, it is only because in his humility he
does not feel that, with important people, his own likes and
dislikes are material: such importance is its own reward, and
can gain no lustre from Geoffrey, who, when the Friar is attacked
by the Summoner, is ready to show him the same sympathy he
shows the Monk (see D1265-67).

Once he has finished describing the really important people
on the pilgrimage the pilgrim's tone changes, for he can now
concern himself with the bourgeoisie, members of his own class
for whom he does not have to show such profound respect. Indeed, he can even afford to be a little patronizing at times, and
have his little joke at the expense of the too-busy lawyer. But
such indirect assertions of his own superiority do not prevent
him from giving substance to the old cynicism that the only

2—S.O.C.

motive recognized by the middle class is the profit motive, for
his interest and admiration for the bourgeois pilgrims is centred
mainly in their material prosperity and their ability to increase
it. He starts, properly enough, with the out-and-out money-
grubber, the Merchant, and after turning aside for that *lusus
naturae*, the non-profit-motivated Clerk, proceeds to the Lawyer,
who, despite the pilgrim's little joke, is the best and best-paid
ever; the Franklin, twenty-one admiring lines on appetite, so
expensively catered to; the Gildsmen, cheered up the social
ladder, 'For catel hadde they ynough and rente' (A373); and the
Physician, again the best and richest. In this series the portrait of
the Clerk is generally held to be an ideal one, containing no
irony; but while it is ideal, it seems to reflect the pilgrim's sense
of values in his joke about the Clerk's failure to make money:
is not this still typical of the half-patronizing, half-admiring
*un*understanding that practical men of business display towards
academics? But in any case the portrait is a fine companion-
piece for those in which material prosperity is the main interest
both of the characters described and of the describer.

Of course, this is not the sole interest of so gregarious—if shy—
a person as Chaucer the pilgrim. Many of the characters have the
additional advantage of being good companions, a faculty that
receives a high valuation in the Prologue. To be good company
might, indeed, atone for certain serious defects of character. Thus
the Shipman, whose callous cruelty is duly noted, seems fairly
well redeemed in the assertion, 'And certainly he was a good
felawe' (A395). At this point an uneasy sensation that even
tongue-in-cheek irony will not compensate for the lengths to
which Chaucer is going in his approbation of this sinister sea-
farer sometimes causes editors to note that *a good felawe* means
'a rascal'. But I can find no evidence that it ever meant a rascal.
Of course, all tritely approbative expressions enter easily into
ironic connotation, but the phrase *means* a good companion,
which is just what Chaucer means. And if, as he says of the
Shipman, 'Of nice conscience took he no keep' (A398), Chaucer
the pilgrim was doing the same with respect to him.

Nothing that has been said has been meant to imply that the
pilgrim was unable to recognise, and deplore, a rascal when he
saw one. He could, provided the rascality was situated in a

member of the lower classes and provided it was, in any case, somewhat wider than a barn door: Miller, Manciple, Reeve, Summoner, and Pardoner are all acknowledged to be rascals. But rascality generally has, after all, the laudable object of making money, which gives it a kind of validity, if not dignity. These portraits, while in them the pilgrim, prioress-like conscious of the finer aspects of life, does deplore such matters as the Miller's indelicacy of language, contain a note of ungrudging admiration for efficient thievery. It is perhaps fortunate for the pilgrim's reputation as a judge of men that he sees through the Pardoner, since it is the Pardoner's particular tragedy that, except in Church, every one can see through him at a glance; but in Church he remains to the pilgrim 'a noble ecclesiaste' (A708). The equally repellent Summoner, a practising bawd, is partially redeemed by his also being a good fellow, 'a gentil harlot and a kinde' (A647), and by the fact that for a moderate bribe he will neglect to summon: the pilgrim apparently subscribes to the popular definition of the best policeman as the one who acts the least policely.

Therefore Chaucer is tolerant, and has his little joke about the Summoner's small Latin—a very small joke, though one of the most amusing aspects of the pilgrim's character is the pleasure he takes in his own jokes, however small. But the Summoner goes too far when he cynically suggests that purse is the Archdeacon's hell, causing Chaucer to respond with a fine show of righteous respect for the instruments of spiritual punishment. The only trouble is that his enthusiastic defence of them carries *him* too far, so that after having warned us that excommunication will indeed damn our souls—

> But wel I woot he lied right in deede:
> Of cursing oughte eech gilty man him drede,
> For curs wol slee right as assoiling savith— (A659-61)

he goes on to remind us that it will also cause considerable inconvenience to our bodies: 'And also war him of a *Significavit*' (A662). Since a *Significavit* is the writ accomplishing the imprisonment of the excommunicate, the line provides perhaps the neatest—and most misunderstood—Chaucerian anticlimax in the Prologue.

I have avoided mentioning, hitherto, the pilgrim's reactions to the really good people on the journey—the Knight, the Parson, the Plowman. One might reasonably ask how his uncertain sense of values may be reconciled with the enthusiasm he shows for their rigorous integrity. The question could, of course, be shrugged off with a remark on the irrelevance to art of exact consistency, even to art distinguished by its verisimilitude. But I am not sure that there is any basic inconsistency. It is the nature of the pilgrim to admire all kinds of superlatives, and the fact that he often admires superlatives devoid of—or opposed to—genuine virtue does not inhibit his equal admiration for virtue incarnate. He is not, after all, a bad man; he is, to place him in his literary tradition, merely an average man, or mankind: *homo*, not very *sapiens* to be sure, but with the very best intentions, making his pilgrimage through the world in search of what is good, and showing himself, too frequently, able to recognize the good only when it is spectacularly so. Spenser's Una glows with a kind of spontaneous incandescence, so that the Red Cross Knight, mankind in search of holiness, knows her as good; but he thinks that Duessa is good, too. Virtue concretely embodied in Una or the Parson presents no problems to the well-intentioned observer, but in a world consisting mostly of imperfections, accurate evaluations are difficult for a pilgrim who, like mankind, is naïve. The pilgrim's ready appreciation for the virtuous characters is perhaps the greatest tribute that could be paid to their virtue, and their spiritual simplicity is, I think, enhanced by the intellectual simplicity of the reporter.

The pilgrim belongs, of course, to a very old—and very new—tradition of the fallible first person singular. His most exact modern counterpart is perhaps Lemuel Gulliver who, in his search for the good, failed dismally to perceive the difference between the pursuit of reason and the pursuits of reasonable horses: one may be sure that the pilgrim would have whinnied with the best of them. In his own century he is related to Long Will of *Piers Plowman*, a more explicit seeker after the good, but just as unswerving in his inability correctly to evaluate what he sees. Another kinsman is the protagonist of the *Pearl*, mankind whose heart is set on a transitory good that has been lost—who, for very natural reasons, confuses earthly with spiritual values.

Not entirely unrelated is the protagonist of Gower's *Confessio Amantis*, an old man seeking for an impossible earthly love that seems to him the only good. And in more subtle fashion there is the teller of Chaucer's story of *Troilus and Criseide*, who, while not a true protagonist, performs some of the same functions. For this unloved 'servant of the servants of love' falls in love with Criseide so persuasively that almost every male reader of the poem imitates him, so that we all share the heartbreak of Troilus and sometimes, in the intensity of our heartbreak, fail to learn what Troilus did. Finally, of course, there is Dante of the *Divine Comedy*, the most exalted member of the family and perhaps the immediate original of these other first-person pilgrims.

Artistically the device of the *persona* has many functions, so integrated with one another that to try to sort them out produces both over-simplification and distortion. The most obvious, with which this paper has been dealing—distortedly, is to present a vision of the social world imposed on one of the moral world. Despite their verisimilitude most, if not all, of the characters described in the Prologue are taken directly from stock and recur again and again in medieval literature. Langland in his own Prologue and elsewhere depicts many of them: the hunting monk, the avaricious friar, the thieving miller, the hypocritical pardoner, the unjust stewards, even, in little, the all-too-human nun. But while Langland uses the device of the *persona* with considerable skill in the conduct of his allegory, he uses it hardly at all in portraying the inhabitants of the social world: these are described directly, with the poet's own voice. It was left to Chaucer to turn the ancient stock satirical characters into real people assembled for a pilgrimage, and to have them described, with all their traditional faults upon them, by another pilgrim who records faithfully each fault without, for the most part, recognizing that it is a fault and frequently felicitating its possessor for possessing it. One result—though not the only result—is a moral realism much more significant than the literary realism which is a part of it and for which it is sometimes mistaken; this moral realism discloses a world in which humanity is prevented by its own myopia, the myopia of the describer, from seeing what the dazzlingly attractive externals of life really represent. In most of the analogues mentioned above the fallible first person receives, at the end of the book, the education he has needed: the pilgrim arrives somewhere. Chaucer never completed the *Canterbury Tales*, but in the Prologue to the Parson's Tale he seems to have been doing, rather hastily, what his contemporaries had done: when, with the sun nine-and-twenty degrees from the horizon, the twenty-nine pilgrims come to a certain—unnamed—*thropes ende* (I12), then the pilgrimage seems no longer to have Canterbury as its destination, but rather, I suspect, the Celestial City of which the Parson speaks.

If one insists that Chaucer was not a moralist but a comic writer (a distinction without a difference), then the device of the *persona* may be taken primarily as serving comedy. It has been said earlier that the several Chaucers must have inhabited one body, and in that sense the fictional first person is no fiction at all. In an oral tradition of literature the first person probably always shared the personality of his creator: thus Dante of the *Divine Comedy* was physically Dante the Florentine; the John Gower of the *Confessio* was also Chaucer's friend John Gower; and Long Will was, I am sure, some one named William Langland, who was both long and wilful. And it is equally certain that Chaucer the pilgrim, 'a popet in an arm t'enbrace' (B1891), was in every physical respect Chaucer the man, whom one can imagine reading his work to a courtly audience, as in the portrait appearing in one of the MSS of *Troilus*. One can imagine also the delight of the audience which heard the Prologue read in this way, and which was aware of the similarities and dissimilarities between Chaucer, the man before them, and Chaucer the pilgrim, both of whom they could see with simultaneous vision. The Chaucer they knew was physically, one gathers, a little ludicrous; a bourgeois, but one who was known as a practical and successful man of the court; possessed perhaps of a certain diffidence of manner, reserved, deferential to the socially imposing persons with whom he was associated; a bit absent-minded, but affable and, one supposes, very good company—a good fellow; sagacious and highly perceptive. This Chaucer was telling them of another who, lacking some of his chief qualities, nevertheless possessed many of his characteristics, though in a different state of balance, and each one probably distorted just enough to become laughable without becoming unrecognizable: deference into a kind of snobbishness, affability into an over-readiness to please, practicality into Babbittry, perception into inspection, absence of mind into dimness of wit; a Chaucer acting in some respects just as Chaucer himself might have acted but unlike his creator the kind of man, withal, who could mistake a group of stock satirical types for living persons endowed with all sorts of superlative qualities. The constant interplay of these two Chaucers must have produced an exquisite and most ingratiating humour—as, to be sure, it still does. This comedy reaches its superb climax when Chaucer the pilgrim, resembling in so many ways Chaucer the poet, can answer the Host's demand for a story only with a rhyme he 'lerned longe agoon' (B1899)—*Sir Thopas*, which bears the same complex relation to the kind of romance it satirizes and to Chaucer's own poetry as Chaucer the pilgrim does to the pilgrims he describes and to Chaucer the poet.

Earlier in this paper I proved myself no gentleman (though I hope a scholar) by being rude to the Prioress, and hence to the many who like her and think that Chaucer liked her too. It is now necessary to retract. Undoubtedly Chaucer the man would, like his fictional representative, have found her charming and looked on her with affection. To have got on so well in so changeable a world Chaucer must have got on well with the people in it, and it is doubtful that one may get on with people merely by pretending to like them: one's heart has to be in it. But the third entity, Chaucer the poet, operates in a realm which is above and subsumes those in which Chaucer the man and Chaucer the pilgrim have their being. In this realm prioresses may be simultaneously evaluated as marvellously amiable ladies and as prioresses. In his poem the poet arranges for the moralist to define austerely what ought to be and for his fictional representative—who, as the representative of all mankind, is no mere fiction—to go on affirming affectionately what is. The two points of view, in strict moral logic diametrically opposed, are somehow made harmonious in Chaucer's wonderfully comic attitude, that double vision that is his ironical essence. The mere critic performs his etymological function by taking the Prioress apart and clumsily separating her good parts from her bad; but the poet's function is to build her incongruous and

inharmonious parts into an inseparable whole which is infinitely greater than its parts. In this complex structure both the
latent moralist and the naïve reporter have important positions, but I am not persuaded that in every case it is possible to
determine which of them has the last word.[1]

[1] Books referred to or cited in this paper are G. L. Kittredge, *Chaucer and His Poetry*
(Cambridge, Mass., 1915), p. 45; Eileen Power, *Medieval People* (London, 1924), pp. 59–
84. Robinson's note to A650 records the opinion that *a good felawe* means a 'rascal'.
The medieval reader's expectation that the first person in a work of fiction would
represent mankind generally and at the same time would physically resemble the
author is commented on by Leo Spitzer in an interesting note in *Traditio*, iv (1946),
414–22.

2

IDIOM OF POPULAR POETRY
IN THE MILLER'S TALE

A POET WHO ABANDONS the poetic idiom of his time and nation and devises one entirely new in its place creates for the would-be critic of his language a difficult problem. Criticism of the language of poetry can exist only through comparison with contemporary and earlier writings, and when, as sometimes happens, the critic cannot find between these and the work of the innovator enough similarity even to reflect the differences, he has to resort, in lieu of criticism, to merely quoting the innovator admiringly. With Chaucer the problem is even greater than with Milton, Shakespeare, Wordsworth, or Eliot. For while we may at least be sure that they were brought up in an English literary tradition from which they more or less consciously revolted, the disquieting suspicion always arises that Chaucer, bred if not born in a culture predominantly continental, may not have been very much aware of the literary tradition from which he was presumably in revolt; and this means that anyone who, in search of comparison with Chaucer's diction, goes to the most prolific of the vernacular literary traditions, the romance, or to the closely related lyric, must consider himself to be in danger of wasting his time.[1]

But Chaucer did, after all, write in English, however continental his background may have been, and it stands to reason that diligent search will reveal at least a few correspondences

[1] The researches of Laura H. Loomis in recent years have, however, done much to justify such comparison by demonstrating Chaucer's familiarity with the native romance tradition. See 'Chaucer and the Auchinleck MS . . .', in *Essays and Studies in Honor of Carleton Brown* (New York, 1940), pp. 111–28; 'Chaucer and the Breton Lays of the Auchinleck MS', *SP*, xxxviii (1941), 14–33; and her study of *Sir Thopas* in *Sources and Analogues* . . . (Chicago, 1941), pp. 486–559.

with the popular English poetic diction of his day. Complete analysis of his own vocabulary is now—and has been for some time—possible through use of the Chaucer *Concordance*; in this one can study all the contexts of every word he ever used, and hence can try to determine the values he placed upon the words he appropriated from the conventional vocabulary of popular poetry. It is the evaluation of these borrowings that I have undertaken; but since the job is a tricky one at best, I have thought it advisable to begin with those words which, while common in contemporary romance and lyric, occur only a very few times in Chaucer and are therefore to be suspected of carrying a rather special sort of weight.

In approaching the problem of evaluation there are two subordinate poems that I have found to be of some help. The first is Fragment A of the Middle English translation of the *Roman de la Rose*. That this is really Chaucer's work cannot be entirely proved. Most scholars think it is,[1] and I have little doubt that it is. But even if it is not, it is at least the sort of poem we should suppose him to have written in his poetic immaturity. For while it is not nearly so free as Chaucer's mature works are from that conventional diction—those clichés—by which the whole vernacular tradition was infected,[2] it nevertheless frequently has that quality, common to all Chaucer's indisputable works, of uniting perfectly simple English words with extraordinary ease into genuinely poetic language of a kind that makes the phrase 'poetic diction' seem entirely too high-flown to be apt. Whether it is by Chaucer or not, its diction, occasionally but not consistently conventional, seems to represent a half-way point between popular English poetry and the *Canterbury Tales*. I find it critically illuminating, therefore, in comparing the Fragment with the *Canterbury Tales*, to observe how the mature Chaucer places in new and sometimes startling contexts words which a poet of somewhat less refined taste (probably the young Chaucer) had used flatly in time-honoured contexts.

Rather firmer help is offered by Chaucer's *Sir Thopas*. For this

[1] For a summary of scholarly opinions on the authorship of the Fragment see Joseph Mersand, *Chaucer's Romance Vocabulary* (New York, 1939), p. 60, n. 7.

[2] See, for instance, the old poetic word 'swire' (neck); and the conventional alliterative phrases *styf in stour* and *byrde in bour*.

parody, while a criticism of vernacular conventions of every sort, is above all a criticism of standard English poetic diction. Therefore, if we find—as we do—words that Chaucer makes fun of in *Sir Thopas* showing up in seemingly innocent contexts elsewhere in his work, we shall have at least a small area in which to exercise criticism of Chaucer's idiom. Let me confess at once that the total critical yield from the words of this sort that I have noticed is not great and that it makes possible, not a wider appreciation of Chaucer's more serious poetry, but of some of his comic effects. In this paper I shall deal largely with the effect upon the Miller's Tale of certain words introduced from the vernacular poetic tradition. It goes almost without saying that this effect is ironical and that more irony is not the sole product I should have wished to achieve from my investigation. Still, this is only a beginning, and 'after this I hope ther cometh more'—if not from me, from better critics. The following is therefore presented as an example of a technique by which it may be possible to arrive at a better understanding of Chaucer's poetic idiom.

Since in the Miller's Tale I shall be dealing with ironical context, I shall start with an illustration of an ironical use of conventional idiom that is, thanks to the brilliant work of Professor Lowes, known to every Chaucerian. Lowes has demonstrated that the key to the portrait of the Prioress is in the second line, which, in describing her smiling as 'ful simple and coy', endows her with a pair of qualities that were also those of innumerable heroines of Old French romance.[1] It is, incidentally, a measure of Chaucer's gallicization, as well as of his tact with a lady who likes to speak at least a sort of French, that these conventional words, along with most of the others in her characterization, are not commonly applied to ladies in Middle English romance. Furthermore, Lowes shows that in describing her person—grey eyes, delicate soft red mouth, fair forehead, nose *tretis*—Chaucer borrows from stock French descriptions of ladies details that were full of courtly reminiscences for the cultivated reader of the time, though with impeccable taste he forgoes the complete physical catalogue that an Old French heroine would feel herself entitled to. If Lowes had wished to reinforce his point,

[1] J. L. Lowes, 'Simple and Coy . . .', *Anglia*, xxxiii (1910), 440–51.

whose delicacy needs no reinforcement, he could have gone on to examine Chaucer's own works for the reappearance of the words used to describe the Prioress. He would have found, for instance, that 'coy' is used of no other woman in Chaucer, though it appears in the stereotype 'as coy as a maid', used only of men. 'Simple', as Lowes does observe, is also the attribute of Blanche the Duchess—Chaucer's most serious conventional portrait; but it is applied further to three romantic ladies in the first fragment of the *Roman*, and, in Chaucer's mature work, it is used twice of Criseide, perhaps in a delicate attempt to be suggestive about her manner without being communicative about her character. It is worthy of note that the Prioress's nose *tretis* is foreshadowed by the face *tretis* of Lady Beauty in the English *Roman*; but the word is otherwise non-Chaucerian. Further, while ladies' noses receive full treatment in the translation of the *Roman*, elsewhere the only female nose mentioned is the stubby one that the miller's daughter inherited from her father in the Reeve's Tale—'With camuse nose, and yën greye as glas', an interesting mutation, incidentally, on the Prioress, 'Hir nose tretis, hir yën greye as glas'. And of all the women in Chaucer, only the Prioress and Alison, heroine of the Miller's Tale, have mouths or foreheads worthy of note: a case, perhaps, of the Colonel's Lady and Judy O'Grady. Finally, if one had time one might, I think, profitably investigate the words 'fetis' and 'fetisly', both used in describing the Prioress, but elsewhere appearing only in contexts which render highly suspect the particular sort of elegance they suggest.[1] In any case, the Prioress's portrait is a masterpiece of idiomatic irony, though the idiom is that of French poetry rather than of English.

With this much preliminary let us turn to the Miller's Tale. Upon this, Chaucer's worst ribaldry, it is generally agreed that he lavished his greatest skill, and in particular upon his description of the three principal characters—Alison, Absolon, and *hende* Nicholas, and upon their dialogue with one another. One of the devices he used most skilfully was that of sprinkling these characterizations and conversations with clichés borrowed from

[1] Aside from Fragment A of the *Roman*, where the words are common, they are normally used only by lower-class speakers; the only exceptions are in the portraits of the Prioress and the Merchant.

the vernacular versions of the code of courtly love—phrases of the sort we are accustomed to meet, on the one hand, in Middle English minstrel romances and, on the other, in secular lyrics such as those preserved in Harley MS 2253—but phrases that are not encountered elsewhere in the serious works of Geoffrey Chaucer. The comic effect of this imported courtly diction will, I hope, be understood as we go along. At the start it is necessary to bear in mind only that by the fourteenth century at least, the aim and end of courtly love was sexual consummation, however idealized it may have been made to appear, and that of the various factors upon which the *ars honeste amandi* depended for its idealization the conventional language associated with it was not the least important.

The key to the matter, as one might expect, is in the constant epithet applied to the hero of the Miller's Tale—that is, in hende Nicholas's almost inseparable *hende*. Any one who has done even cursory reading in popular English poetry of Chaucer's time— and before and after—will heartily agree with the *Oxford Dictionary*'s statement that 'hende' is 'a conventional epithet of praise, very frequent in Middle English poetry'. Originally it seems to have meant no more than 'handy, at hand'; but it gradually extended its area of signification to include the ideas of 'skilful, clever' and of 'pleasant, courteous, gracious' (or 'nice', as the *Oxford Dictionary* says with what I take to be exasperated quotation marks); and it simultaneously extended its area of reference to include, under the general sense 'nice', almost every hero and heroine, as well as most of the rest of the characters siding with the angels, in Middle English popular poetry. Thus, the right of the Squire of Low Degree to the hand of the King's Daughter of Hungary is established by the minstrel poet's exclamation:

> The squir was curteous and hend,
> Ech man him loved and was his frend.

And another poet boasts of Sir Isumbras,

> Alle hym loffede, that hym seghe:
> So hende a man was hee![1]

[1] *Squyr of Lowe Degre*, ed. Mead, ll. 3–4; *Sir Ysumbras*, ed. Schleich, ll. 17–18; for examples of many of the characteristics discussed here, see W. C. Curry, *The Middle English Ideal of Personal Beauty* (Baltimore, 1916).

Such examples could be multiplied indefinitely. Indeed, the average popular poet could no more do without 'hende' than he could do without the lovers whose endless misadventures gave him his plots, since unless a lover was 'hende', he or she was no proper exponent of courtly love. We should, therefore, have a right to expect the adjective to modify such Chaucerian characters as Troilus and Criseide, Arveragus and Dorigen, Palamon, Arcite, and Emily. But in Chaucer's indisputable works the word, while it is used eleven times with Nicholas, appears only twice elsewhere, and it is applied to none of the more serious characters, such as those just mentioned. The translator of Fragment A of the *Roman* had, to be sure, used it twice to describe amiable folk associated with the garden of the Rose; but thereafter it is spoken only by the Host, that distinguished exponent of bourgeois good manners, when he calls upon the Friar to be 'hende' to the Summoner; and by Alice of Bath, who expresses with it the charm possessed by her fifth-husband-to-be, jolly Jankin, who is a spiritual sibling of Nicholas's if there ever was one. It is clear from these usages, as well as from the even more eloquent lack of its use in any genuinely courtly context, that for Chaucer 'hende' had become so *déclassé* and shopworn as to be ineligible for employment in serious poetry.

But by the same token it was highly eligible for employment in the Miller's Tale. Nicholas is, after all, a hero of sorts, and he deserves to be as 'hende' as any other self-respecting hero-lover. But in the present context the word mocks the broad meaning 'nice' that is apparent in non-Chaucerian contexts. Indeed, its constant association with Nicholas encourages one to feel that here 'hende' does not so much define Nicholas as he defines it. Furthermore, he defines it in a way that is surprisingly true to the less usual senses of the word, for Nicholas turns out to be a good deal less romantically 'nice' than he is realistically 'clever, skilful'. He even represents the earliest meaning of the word, 'at hand, handy'; for the Miller, analyzing his love-triangle in proverbial terms, remarks that always the 'nye slye' (the sly dog at hand, Nicholas) displaces the 'ferre leve' (the distant charmer, Absolon). But most important, in Nicholas as in other heroes, the quality of being 'hende' is the cause of his success in love. In the quotations given above we learn that it was because

they were 'hende' that Sir Isumbras and the Squire of Low Degree were generally beloved. Nicholas is also lovable, but his
lovableness is of the rather special sort that would appeal to a
woman of Alison's tastes and morals. In short, the coupling of
word and character suggests in Nicholas nothing more than a
large measure of physical charm that is skilful at recognizing
its opportunities and putting itself to practical sexual use; and
this is a sorry degradation for an adjective that had been accustomed to modify some of the nicest people in popular poetry,
who now, as a result of Nicholas, begin to suffer from guilt by
association.

A somewhat similar aspect of Nicholas's character is reflected
in the line that tells us,

> Of derne love he coude, and of solas. (A3200)

For his aptitude at *derne love*, 'secret love', Nicholas must have
been the envy of a good many young men in contemporary
English poetry. For instance, in the Harley MS we meet several
swains whose unsuccessful involvement in secret love affairs is
their chief source of poetic woe.

> Lutel wot hit any mon
> hou derne loue may stonde,

grumbles one of these before going on to explain with what
agonies and ecstasies it is attended.[1] Such lyricists were probably
apt to pretend to themselves that the secretive line of conduct
suggested by the phrase 'derne love', while it may have made
things difficult, was nevertheless one of the ennobling conditions
imposed upon them by the courtly code. Chaucer, however,
seems to have felt otherwise, for while many of his heroes experience 'secree love', none besides Nicholas is ever 'derne'
about it. Elsewhere Chaucer does not even use the common
adjective to modify other nouns besides 'love', apparently feeling that its reputation had been ruined by the company it had
kept so long. Even in Old English, of course, the word was ambiguous, reflecting sometimes justified secrecy and sometimes
secret sin; and among the moral lyrics of the Harley MS there is

---

[1] See *The Harley Lyrics*, ed. G. L. Brook (Manchester, 1948), 32.1–2; also 3.36 and
9.43 (references are to poem and line numbers).

one whose author makes it clear that for him 'derne dedes' are dirty deeds.[1] From his avoidance of the adjective it appears that Chaucer also subscribed to such an opinion. Moreover, the modern reader of the Harley love lyrics will probably sympathize with him, for it sometimes seems that, whatever the lovers pretended, they respected the principle of 'derne love' more because of its value in protecting them from outraged husbands or fathers than from any courtly ideal of preserving their lady's good name.[2] Thus, long before Chaucer's time 'derne love' was already in potentiality what it becomes in actuality in Nicholas, a device for getting away with adultery, if not really a sort of excuse for indulging in it. Therefore Nicholas's aptitude parodies an ideal already devalued through misuse in the vernacular; and since even at its most exalted the courtly code of secrecy might be described as crassly practical, his aptitude also parodies that of more genuinely courtly lovers than the Harley lyricists.

Turning to Nicholas's rival, jolly Absolon, one may find further instances of this technique of Chaucer's. What Absolon lacks in the way of Nicholas's 'hendeness' he tries to make up with his own 'joly-ness'. The epithet 'joly' is not as consistently used with Absolon as 'hende' is with Nicholas, and since it has a wide variety of meanings and is common in Chaucer, it may not be so readily classified. Suffice it to say that it is generally in the mouths of bourgeois characters and that in the senses 'handsome' and 'pretty' it modifies men or women with equal frequency. But it is, perhaps, the secret of Absolon's ill-success that all his jollification makes rather for prettiness than for masculine effectiveness. One recalls that Sir Thopas, though a sturdy hero, possesses some of the charms of a typical medieval heroine, and the Miller seems to suggest by several of the terms in his portrait of Absolon that the latter had somehow or other fallen across the fine line which in medieval poetry separated feminine beauty from that of beardless youths. For in his description he uses words that a minstrel poet would normally apply to a pretty girl. For instance,

His rode was reed, his yën greye as goos, (A3317)

[1] See *OED*, dern, and Brook, 2.5–11.
[2] See Brook, 24.17–20.

and the grey eyes will remind us of the Prioress, as well as of countless other medieval heroines and, it must be granted, a number of heroes, though not in Chaucer, who reserves grey eyes for ladies. But in possessing a 'rode'—that is, a peaches-and-cream complexion recommended by fourteenth-century Elizabeth Ardens, Absolon places himself in the almost exclusive company of Middle English damsels.[1] The complexion of truly manly males of the time was, after all, generally obscured by a good deal of beard, and hence apt to remain unsung. It is significant that the only other 'rode' in all Chaucer belongs to Sir Thopas, a feminine feature that contrasts startlingly with the saffron beard of that curiously constituted creature. Absolon further distinguishes himself (from his sex, I fear) by being the only character in Chaucer to be associated with the adjective 'lovely', which is applied to the looks he casts upon the ladies of the parish and to no other thing Chaucerian, though to hundreds of things, especially things feminine, in popular poetry.[2]

Readers of the latter would naturally expect the flesh of this pretty fellow to be

As whit as is the blosme upon the ris, (A3324)

and it comes as a surprise that it is not Absolon's flesh, but his surplice, that is described in these terms. But the line, either in much the same form or, if one wants pink flesh, with the variation 'as reed as rose on ris', is one of the clichés found almost inevitably in descriptions of women.[3] For instance, the variant form is applied to Lady Beauty's flesh in the *Roman* fragment. But in what we are sure is Chaucer's work there is elsewhere no such phrase—indeed, there is elsewhere no such thing as a 'ris', 'spray', at all. When he quietly transfers the conventional descriptive phrase from the body to the clothing that covers it—in this case Absolon's surplice—Chaucer is, of course, creating the humour of surprise; but more important, the trick enables him

---

[1] For examples see Curry, pp. 92–94. In contexts not concerned with romantic love or lovers this word, as well as others discussed here, was commonly employed without regard to gender.

[2] For an example see Brook, 14.32. *OED, lovely*, records the word at *Anel* 142, but Skeat and Robinson read 'lowly'.

[3] Curry, p. 94; also Brook, 3.11, 5.32.

3—S.O.C.

to evoke for the reader the hackneyed context, with all its associations, in which the phrase usually appears, while at the same time the poet can make literal use of the phrase's meaning in his own more realistic description. There is an even more effective example of this economy in the portrait of Alison, to which I shall now turn.

The pretty heroine of the tale exemplifies most brilliantly Chaucer's reduction of the worn-out ideal, expressed by the worn-out phrase, to its lowest common denominator of sexuality.

> Fair was this yonge wif, and therwithal
> As any wesele hir body gent and smal. (A3233-4)

Now the weasel, as Lowes has observed,[1] is Chaucer's own fresh image, and its effectiveness is obvious. But the fact that Alison's body is 'gent and smal'—shapely and delicate—makes her the sister of every contemporary vernacular heroine who is worthy of having a lover.[2] Lady Beauty, paragon of embraceable women in the *Roman*, is in a similar way shapely (l. 1032)—

> Gente, and in hir myddill small—

and it is natural that Sir Thopas should be 'fair and gent'. Possibly with Sir Thopas 'gent' has its non-physical sense of 'high-born, noble', but in view of the fact that the poet later commends his 'sides smale'—an item of female beauty—one may detect in the word at least a suggestion of ambiguity. On the other hand, while many lovely women in Chaucer's known works are 'gentil', none besides Alison is 'gent'. His third and last use of the adjective is in the *Parliament of Fowls*, where it describes, appropriately enough, the 'facounde gent', the 'noble' eloquence, of the down-to-earth goose (a sort of female Miller in feathers) who speaks so uncourtly of the tercel eagles' love dilemma. Thus, in applying the stale adjective 'gent' to Alison's body the Miller seems to be regarding her from a point of view less ideal and aesthetic than realistic and pragmatic.

As in the case of the Prioress, Chaucer's restraint (I suspect that here it is only a teasing sort of restraint) prevents him from listing—except for one startling detail—the other conventional

---

[1] *Geoffrey Chaucer* (Oxford, 1934), p. 177.
[2] Curry, p. 102.

charms of Alison's body. We might expect from the Miller that our heroine would be—as Lowes has said—'anatomized in good set similes as inescapable as death', as, for instance, is Annot of the Harley lyric 'Annot and John'.[1] But the reader who wants this is doomed to disappointment, for what he gets is less of Alison's body than of her wardrobe. Several of the conventional terms, however, that one expects to meet in corporeal catalogues are still present, even though they are applied only to her clothing. Her sides, to be sure, are not like the Harley Fair Maid of Ribblesdale's,

> Whittore then the moren-mylk,[2]

but her apron is, a quality it shares in Chaucer only with the silk purse of the pink-and-white fleshed Franklin. This same apron lies, moreover,

> Upon hir lendes, ful of many a gore. (A3237)

Now 'gore', which meant originally a triangular piece of land and later (as here) a triangular strip of cloth, hence by synecdoche a skirt or apron, is obviously a technical word, and the fact that Chaucer used it only twice may not be significant. But when one recalls the number of vernacular ladies—including Alison's namesake in the Harley lyrics—who were 'geynest vnder gore', or 'glad vnder gore',[3] one may, perhaps, become suspicious. To be sure, scholars assure us that these phrases, along with such variants as 'worthy under wede', 'lovesome under line', 'semely under serk', are merely stereotyped superlatives and presumably have no sexual connotation.[4] But in their literal meanings they could have such a connotation, and in their origin they probably did have. For instance, the poet of *Gawain and the Green Knight* speaks of the lady of the castle as 'lufsum vnder lyne' only when Gawain is being subjected by her to the most powerful sexual temptation. And inasmuch as Chaucer, violating his self-imposed restraint, takes pains to mention the 'lendes' (the loins), a word that appears a little later in a frankly sexual

---

[1] See Lowes, *Geoffrey Chaucer*, loc. cit.; Brook, 3.11–20.

[2] Brook, 7.77; also Curry, p. 81.

[3] Brook, 4.37, 3.16.

[4] See *OED*, gore, sb. 2, 2; *Sir Gawain and the Green Knight*, ed. Tolkien and Gordon (rev. ed., Oxford, 1930), note on l. 1814.

context[1]—that are hidden beneath the 'gores' of Alison's apron,
it is possible that his employment of the word 'gore' is evocative
as well as technical; that he is, indeed, by providing a sort of
realistic paraphrase of the conventional expression, insinuating
what the lover of the Harley Alison really had in mind when he
called his mistress 'geynest vnder gore'. This is only a possibility,
and I should not want to insist upon it. But the possibility becomes stronger when we recall Chaucer's other use of the word[2]
—in Sir Thopas' dream,

> An elf-queene shal my lemman be
> And sleepe under my gore. (B[2]1978–9)

Whatever 'gore' means here—presumably cloak—its context is
unmistakable.

Nowhere does Chaucer's idiom devaluate with more devastating effect the conventional ideal to the level of flat reality than in
two sentences occurring near the end of Alison's portrait. Like
many a lyric and romance poet the Miller discovers that he is not
clever enough to describe the total effect his lady produces—
indeed, he doubts that any one is clever enough. The poet of the
Life of Ipomedon was later to remark of a lady,

> In all this world is non so wyse
> That hir goodnesse kan devyse,

while the Harley Alison's lover had already asserted,

> In world nis non so wyter mon
> That al hire bounte telle con.[3]

True to the convention, the Miller exclaims of his Alison,

> In al this world, to seeken up and down,
> There nis no man so wis that coude thenche
> So gay a popelote, or swich a wenche. (A3252–4)

But the Miller's mind is not on the 'bounte' (excellence) or
'goodnesse' of Alison; and his crashing anticlimax, ending with
the word 'wenche', which, in Chaucer, when it does not mean

---

[1] 'And (Nicholas) thakked hire upon the lendes weel.'

[2] In MS Harley 7334, A3322 reads: 'Schapen with goores in the newe get', which
Tatlock regarded as a possible Chaucerian revision: see Robinson's textual note on
the line.

[3] Lyfe of Ipomydon, ed. Koelbing, ll. 123–24; Brook, 4.26–27.

servant-girl means a slut,[1] is a triumph of the whole process we have been examining. Another occurs a little later. Once more the Miller is following convention, this time comparing Alison to a flower. John had said of Annot in the Harley lyric,

> The primerole he passeth, the peruenke of pris,[2]

and the Miller also begins his comparison with the cowslip, the 'primerole':

> She was a primerole, a piggesnye. (A3268)

But the accompanying item is no longer a 'peruenke of pris', an excellent periwinkle, but a 'piggesneye', something which, while it may be also a flower (perhaps, appropriately enough, a cuckoo flower),[3] remains, unmistakably, a pig's eye. Beneath the Miller's remorseless criticism the Blanchefleurs and even the Emilys of Middle English romance degenerate into the complacent targets of a lewd whistle.

In their conversation with Alison the two clerks talk like a couple of Harley lyricists.[4] But Absolon, fated to accomplish more words than deeds, naturally has the richer opportunity to speak in the vernacular of love—or rather, to quote Absolon, of love-longing.

[1] In his thorough study of the dialect of the Reeve's Tale in *Transactions of the Philological Society* (London) for 1934, p. 52, Tolkien observes that 'wench' 'was still a respectable and literary word for "girl" in Chaucer's time, and was probably in pretty general use all over the country.' But it was not a respectable word in Chaucer's eyes (except in the sense 'servant-girl'), as a study of his uses will quickly reveal; see the Manciple's definition, H211–22.

[2] Brook, 3.13; cf. 14.51–53.

[3] See Manly's note, citing an *English Dialect Dictionary* definition for Essex, in his edition of the *Canterbury Tales* (New York, 1928), p. 560.

[4] One is frequently tempted to suggest that Chaucer had the Harley lyrics in mind as he wrote the Miller's Tale, but in view of the adverse conditions for the preservation of secular lyrics, to associate Chaucer with a few survivals seems too large an economy. Particularly close correspondences may be noted with the lyric 'De Clerico et Puella' (Brook, 24), a dramatic dialogue in which a maiden initially repulses a clerk's plea of secret love: notice especially the third stanza, where she rebukes him ('Do wey, thou clerc, thou art a fol') and warns him of the consequences if he should be caught in her bower, and compare Alison's initial resistance ('Do way youre handes') and her warning (A3294–7); further, the Harley lyric's window where the two had kissed 'fyfty sythe' (l. 23), and the carpenter's shot-window. But the situation is, of course, a very old one (see *Dame Sirith*), and the Harley lyric may go back remotely to the same source from which Chaucer's immediate source stems.

> Ywis, lemman, I have swich love-longinge,
> That lik a turtle trewe is my moorninge, (A3705-6)

he laments outside her window. Love-longing was, of course, a common complaint, positively epidemic in the Middle Ages, and most of Chaucer's lovers have at least occasional attacks of it. But as with certain modern diseases, its name seems to have varied with the social status of its victim, and in Chaucer only Absolon and Sir Thopas are afflicted with it under that name. They are therefore in a tradition that includes knights as illustrious as Sir Tristram, not to mention those rustics the Harley lovers,[1] but fails to include Aurelius, Arcite, Troilus, or even the less admirable Damian. The inference is that for Chaucer the phrase 'love-longing' implied a desire of the flesh irreconcilable with courtly idealism, though fine for Absolon. Absolon is also following popular tradition when he introduces the figure of the legendarily amorous turtle-dove into his declaration: 'like a turtle true is my mourning'. Ordinarily, however, it is the lady who is the dove, a 'trewe tortle in a tour'[2]—faithful and remote in her tower, but curiously inarticulate, considering that she is a dove and that doves are rarely silent. Thus, the conventional image is reset in a context that is more natural and in this case more genuinely poetic. Another simile of Absolon's for conveying his distress—

> I moorne as dooth a lamb after the tete (A3704)

is the Miller's own audacious contribution to the language of love, and demonstrates the ease with which Chaucer, employing a sort of merciless logic, can move from a wholly conventional image involving animals to one wholly original and wholly devastating.

Elsewhere, Absolon keeps closer to what we should expect. Alison, for instance, is his 'swete brīd' or 'brīd'—that is, his sweet bird, bride, or possibly even 'burd' (maiden): as in the romances and love lyrics it is often difficult to tell which of the three the lover means, or whether he is himself altogether sure.[3] In the

---

[1] See Brook, 4.5 *Sir Tristram*, ed. Koelbing, l. 1860.   [2] Brook, 3.22; cf. 9.3.

[3] The Harley lyrics have 'burde', maiden (Brook, 3.1, 5.36), 'brudes', maidens (6.39), 'brid', maiden? (14.17), and 'brid', bird for maiden (6.40). In the *King's Quair*, stanza 65, 'bridis' rhymes with 'bydis' (abides), but clearly means 'birds'.

other works of Chaucer birds are clearly birds, brides clearly brides, and 'burd' does not occur except once of a lady in the *Roman*. Perhaps, however, it is only fair to observe that Chaucer's avoidance elsewhere of this trite form of endearment results in a use of 'dear heart' and of the substantive 'sweete' so excessive as to amount to a triteness of Chaucer's own devising.

Continuing in the lyrical tradition even after the shame of his débacle, Absolon calls Alison his 'derelyng'—the only instance in Chaucer of this indestructible term.[1] But Absolon's lyricism reaches its highest point, naturally, before his disillusionment when, close to what he mistakes for the Promised Land—in this case the shot-window of the carpenter's bower—he begs for Alison's favours—that is, for her 'ore' (mercy), as lyric poets usually expressed it. A Harley poet describing a similar crisis in his relations with his mistress reports,

> Adoun y fel to hire anon
> Ant cri[d]e, "Ledy, thyn ore!"[2]

And much earlier, according to Giraldus Cambrensis, a priest of Worcestershire had so far forgotten himself at the altar as to displace the liturgical response 'Dominus vobiscum' with the lyrical refrain 'Swete lamman, dhin are'.[3] Thus, Absolon was conforming to a very old tradition when, about to receive his kiss, he

> down sette him on his knees,
> And saide, 'I am a lord at alle degrees;
> For after this I hope ther cometh more:
> Lemman, thy grace, and sweete brid, thyn ore!' (A3723-6)

'Ore', the venerable word that is so often in the mouths of lovesick swains in Middle English, occurs in Chaucer only here. And the immediate similarity but impending difference between Absolon's situation and the situation of the average lyric lover epitomizes the technique we have been examining.

One final illustration of Chaucer's use—or abuse—of conventional idiom will suffice. Every reader of medieval romance knows that sooner or later the poet is going to describe a feast,

---

[1] See, for instance, *William of Palerne*, ed. Skeat, l. 1538.
[2] Brook, 32.16-17.
[3] *Opera*, ed. J. S. Brewer, ii (London, 1862), 120.

if not a literal feast of food, at least a metaphorical one of love; and readers of English romances, including, in this case, Chaucer's own, can anticipate with some accuracy the terms in which the feast is going to be described—all the mirth and minstrelsy, or mirth and solace, or bliss and solace, or bliss and revelry, or revelry and melody by which the occasion will be distinguished. In the Miller's Tale the feast is, of course, of the metaphorical kind, consisting in the consummation of an adulterous love; and the obscene Miller, with his vast talent for realism, adapts the hackneyed old phrases most aptly to the situation. The carpenter, snug if uncomfortable in his kneading trough on high, is alternating groans with snores—'for his head mislay'—while Alison and Nicholas are in his bed below.

> Ther was the revel and the melodye,
> And thus lith Alison and Nicholas
> In bisinesse of mirthe and of solas. (A3652–4)

At this feast the carpenter's snores furnish the 'melodye', while his wife and her lover experience the 'solas'—that seemingly innocent word for delight which here receives the full force of Chaucer's genius for devaluation—the completion of a logical process that began when we first heard it said of 'hende' Nicholas that

> Of derne love he coude and of solas.

It is, of course, true that the idiom I have been examining is just what we should expect of the Miller's cultural background —and of that of his characters[1]—and it would be possible to dispose of it by simply labelling it 'verisimilitude'. But verisimilitude seems to me among the least important of artistic criteria, and I refuse to believe that the courtly idiom in the Miller's Tale accomplishes nothing more than that. Perhaps I should have made a larger effort than I have to distinguish the Miller from Chaucer, and my interchanging of their names must have grated on some ears. But as I see it, much of Chaucer's irony in

---

[1] According to L. A. Haselmayer, 'The Portraits in Chaucer's Fabliaux', *RES*, xiv (1938), 310–14, conventionalized portraits existed—though in only a vestigial form—in the French fabliaux with which Chaucer was acquainted. It was perhaps from these that Chaucer got the idea of using conventional poetic idiom in ironic contexts.

the *Canterbury Tales* becomes operative in the no man's land that exists between the poet Chaucer—who if he read his poems aloud must have been a very personal fact to his own audience—and the assigned teller of the tale, whether the Miller, the Knight, or, in *Sir Thopas*, Chaucer the pilgrim. The irony produced by the use of popular poetic idiom in the Miller's Tale becomes operative in this no man's land and operates in several directions. First, the idiom tends to make of the tale a parody of the popular romance, rather like *Sir Thopas* in effect, though less exclusively literary. Then, too, it reinforces the connection between the Miller's Tale and the Knight's truly courtly romance that the Miller's Tale is intended to 'quite' (to repay); for it emphasizes the parallelism between the two different, though somehow similar, love-rivalries, one involving two young knights in remote Athens, the other two young clerks in contemporary Oxford. And in so far as it does this, it tends to turn the tale into a parody of all courtly romance, the ideals of which are subjected to the harshly naturalistic criticism of the fabliau. But finally, while doing its bit in the accomplishment of these things, the idiom Chaucer borrows from popular poetry contributes to the directly humorous effect of the Miller's Tale and that is probably its chief function.[1]

[1] Since this was written, Fr. Paul E. Beichner has in a delightful paper fully demonstrated the effeminacy of Absolon and its traditional nature; see 'Absolon's Hair', *Mediaeval Studies*, xii (1950), 222–33.

3

THE EFFECT OF THE MERCHANT'S TALE

ONE OF THE MOST PROFOUND and perhaps most significant of the recent disagreements among Chaucerians concerns the tone of the Merchant's Tale. Is this story, as Tatlock[1] and many of the older critics have held, a dark one, filled with bitterness and disgust for the human race as represented by January and May and Damian? Or is it, as several recent writers believe, a merry jest, the humour of which is entirely characteristic of the fabliau genre—something that will, as one critic supposes, make us 'glad'?[2] Some years ago at approximately the same time that Professor Bronson was lightly dismissing the tale as just 'another high card in the unending Game between the Sexes',[3] another Chaucerian was writing that in it 'the dam has given way, and the ugly muck that formerly lay hidden beneath the surface'—presumably of the Merchant's personality—'is exposed to the sight of all'.[4] While this is obviously an overstatement, as well as an overwrought statement, I continue to believe in its sense, even though I now deplore the rankness of its rhetorical colouring. Faced with two such divergent opinions, the student who had never read Chaucer but only Chaucerians—dreary fate—might well conclude that Professor Bronson and I were talking about different stories, or else that one or both of us had not read the Merchant's Tale very well if at all.

[1] J. S. P. Tatlock, 'Chaucer's Merchant's Tale', *MP*, xxxiii (1936), 367–81. This is the classic statement of the older view.

[2] T. W. Craik, *The Comic Tales of Chaucer* (London, 1964), p. 153.

[3] B. H. Bronson, 'Afterthoughts on *The Merchant's Tale*', *SP*, lviii (1961), 596. A similar point of view is expressed by R. M. Jordan, 'The Non-Dramatic Disunity of the Merchant's Tale', *PMLA*, lxxviii (1963), 293–9.

[4] *Chaucer's Poetry*, p. 921.

This kind of divergency of opinion is doubtless due to our both writing descriptive criticism, which means that while we both pretend to be describing the tale objectively, we are in fact describing our reactions to it: we are casting on its persons and incidents a kind of spotlight, to be sure, but one that takes its colouring from our own preconceptions, and these neither of us has troubled to justify to the reader. Thus Professor Bronson succeeds in making everything about the tale sound extremely funny, although he admits that it takes on a certain amount of bitterness because of the characterization of its narrator as an extremely bilious, misogynistic man. On the other hand, I make the same things sound very grim indeed, although I am careful to say, if not to show, that they are somehow very funny. In this paper I should like to try better to justify my feeling that the Merchant's Tale is in truth a grim thing by examining some of the passages that form the basis for my feeling.

First let me try to chase away two red herrings that are constantly stealing the bait from those who fish for literary values in the murky waters of this particular narrative. The first is the general problem of the comic as opposed to the serious in literature. Every one is, of course, aware that the fact that a literary work is funny does not rule out its being highly serious—does not rule out its being, sometimes, as profound a commentary on human life as the most overt tragedy. To put it briefly, laughter is not by necessity thoughtless. I have to repeat this truism because any one who tries to emphasize the darker side of a humorous tale becomes a ready victim of the quick *ad hominem* rebuttal which blurs the distinction between *serious* meaning 'solemn' and *serious* meaning 'important'. 'Ho, ho, ho', the opposition chortles, 'the poor fellow doesn't realize that it's all just a joke'—and, of course, to be caught missing a joke is to forfeit one's respectability as a critic: I'm afraid many of us have been guilty at one time or another of demonstrating our critical superiority by finding jokes in Chaucer's text that our opponents have missed—sometimes, indeed, jokes that Chaucer himself may have missed. But I hope in this paper I may be allowed to talk about the Merchant's Tale without being unduly self-conscious that I am neglecting the obvious fact that it is very funny, in a sad sort of way. In return, I shall apologize to the critic whom I cited rather derisively as having said that the tale is one that will make us glad; any profound work of literature makes one glad, and I am as glad of the Merchant's Tale as he—though not, I confess, immediately after I have finished reading it, when my feeling is aptly expressed by the Host: 'Ey, Goddes mercy!'

The second point needing preliminary discussion is more limited in scope. Only twenty-three of the fifty-two MSS containing the Merchant's Tale include the Merchant's Prologue,[1] in which the Merchant is characterized (for the first time) as an embittered bridegroom. This has led to a good deal of speculation about Chaucer's original intention with regard to the tale, and provides Professor Bronson with one of the bases for his argument that Chaucer wrote it not for a bilious Merchant, but to be told *in propria persona*, from his own mouth, whence it would presumably have come with merry humour devoid of bitterness. Yet when MSS offer several alternatives, one of which characterizes a narrator in a way appropriate to the tale while the others either adapt a link universally admitted to have been written by Chaucer for some one else (in this case, the Franklin)[2] or else make no advance assignment at all, it is only common sense to assume that the more satisfactory alternative represents Chaucer's intention. The frequent absence of the Merchant's Prologue from the MSS may indeed suggest the possibility that Chaucer added it to an already completed (and circulated) tale, but it by no means establishes a probability that he did so: we simply do not know enough about the early history of the copying of the *Canterbury Tales* to feel secure in the belief that the absence of the Merchant's Prologue represents a genuine authorial variant as opposed to a mere scribal one. And even if the variant does represent an earlier phase of authorial intention, since it is clear that Chaucer wrote the appropriate Merchant's Prologue that is preserved in twenty-three MSS, then the variant is important only to a study of Chaucer's method of composition and not to the criticism of the Merchant's Tale as it now stands. Only if, as a literary fact, the tale failed to fit the narrator as he is characterized in its prologue would the existence

[1] See M-R, iii, 374.
[2] M-R, iv, 31.

of other MS alternatives to the prologue become significant, and only provided that among these alternatives was a more satisfactory reading. But not even Professor Bronson denies the suitability of the Merchant's Tale to the Merchant as he is characterized in what is an undeniably authentic prologue. He merely seems to regret it because of the preconceptions he entertains about the kind of poetry that witty, urbane, genial Chaucer ought to have written.

Specifically, he believes that the assignment of the tale to the Merchant, as well as the composition of the Merchant's Prologue (admittedly an unexpected but surely not impossible extension of his portrait in the General Prologue) took place well after the composition of the tale itself. Here is Professor Bronson's statement of the consequences of his belief:[1]

... what the poet may not at once have realized is that the explanation he had provided [that is, the Merchant's Prologue] worked an instant sea-change on the story itself. The Merchant's misogyny impregnated the whole piece with a mordant venom, inflaming what originally had been created for the sake of mirth. That Chaucer could have foreseen this effect is very unlikely.

It is not unfair to say that a good deal more bitterness has been let into the Merchant's Tale by this paragraph, which is near the end of Professor Bronson's article, than one would have expected from his earlier argument. And I will surely allow the point that the 'Merchant's misogyny impregnate[s] the whole piece with a mordant venom'—obviously, that's why the misogyny has been so lovingly presented in the Merchant's Prologue. But since I do not believe in art by inadvertence, I cannot see how Chaucer could not have been aware of what would happen when he assigned a certain kind of tale to a certain kind of narrator: he was after all a master of the art of manipulating and multiplying fictional contexts. But even though I cannot help gasping at Professor Bronson's wholly unsupported (and unsupportable) statement that it is 'unlikely' that Chaucer foresaw the effect he in fact achieved, it is not my present purpose to defend the poet from inexplicable slanders on his artistic intelligence. What I wish to do is to show that it is idle to speculate, in a complete absence of respectable evidence, about when

[1] *SP*, lviii (1961), 596.

Chaucer did what with the Merchant's Tale, since it is a literary fact that it is an intensely bitter story, which, while it suits perfectly its intensely bitter narrator, would of itself, even if it had never been assigned to a specific Canterbury pilgrim, have characterized its narrator as one whose vision was limited almost exclusively to the dark side of things.

The most obvious feature of the Merchant's Tale is its juxtaposition of the seemingly, or potentially, beautiful with the unmistakably ugly, of the 'faire, fresshe' May with the 'olde' January. This juxtaposition of beautiful and ugly is not static but dynamic, for the ugly constantly casts its shadow over the beautiful or, conversely, the seemingly beautiful ultimately reveals itself to be as ugly, in its own way, as that with which it is juxtaposed. Moreover, the main juxtaposition is reflected in all the story's incidents and throughout the details of its poetic style. If I may use a somewhat metaphysical metaphor, the central situation of the story is like the sun suffering eclipse: during a solar eclipse, every bright patch of sunlight screened through a natural filter such as foliage at each moment exactly reproduces the phase of the sun's darkening, so that the ground under leafy trees is covered with hundreds of tiny eclipses, and every sunny spot suffers the encroachment of the shadow. And everywhere within the tale the shadow encroaches. The narrator's (and narrative's) bitterness is such that it goes beyond the inevitable anti-Platonism of the selfish disillusioned romanticist almost to a complete denial of the possibility of any human value: not only is what is beautiful, and hence what one wants to believe good, actually ugly, but even those things that are generally accepted unquestioningly as valuable are either made to seem fatally flawed or are tainted by the Merchant's poison.

The central juxtaposition and its myriad concomitant reflections are handled with what might be called perfectly bad taste. I'm not sure that this isn't just as difficult an artistic effect to achieve as perfectly good taste, for it often consists, not of a piling up of vulgarities, but of the introduction into a relatively innocuous passage of a single, carefully selected vulgarity that will produce an aesthetic shock upon the reader, destroying a context which seemed fair, or one which he at least wanted to believe was fair. The poem is thus constantly affronting our aesthetic sense, bringing our emotions into play in such a way as to confuse our moral judgment, which finds no safe place to settle. The distinctive tone of the Merchant's Tale becomes clear when one compares it, in plot summary, with the Miller's: two succulent young females, May and Alison, married to two variants of the type *senex amans*, January and John, and assorted would-be lovers; and, in the plot summary, two vulgar climaxes, with the Miller's potentially more shocking to the reader than the Merchant's. Yet the drunken Miller has in his own way perfect taste, and his narration of a most vulgar event, Absolon's kissing of Alison's rump, is done with a kind of high-poetic awe—almost as if he were exclaiming, 'What hath God wrought?'—that at once heightens the comedy and diminishes offensiveness. On the other hand, the Merchant, excusing with a mealy apology the baldness of his language, succeeds in making a long-anticipated act of coition seem extremely shocking.

'Healthy animality': I detest the patronizing term, but can't think of a better one to describe the Miller's Tale in its relation to the Merchant's, to which one may apply the modification, 'mere bestiality'. Notice the following lines, January's prospectus for a wife:

> 'I wol noon old wif han in no manere;
> She shal nat passe sixteen yeer certain—
> Old fissh and yong flessh wol I have fain.
> Bet is,' quod he, 'a pik than a pikerel,
> And bet than old boef is the tendre veel:
> I wol no womman thritty yeer of age—
> It is but bene-straw and greet forage.' (E1416–22)

Here January, in the guise of a gourmet who knows all about *la bonne cuisine* whether fish, flesh, or female, is already, if unwittingly, seeing his future wife as the young beast he actually gets. And, as so often happens in the tale, the images the speaker uses catch him up in their own truth. Thus in the last line, the *beanstraw* and *great forage* are, of course, foods not for a *bon vivant*, but for what he is unconsciously admitting himself to be: that is, they are coarse, dry fodder for an old beast stable-bound by winter,[1] which is what January is despite his colt's tooth. And

---

[1] See *OED, forage,* sb. 1; *great,* adj., A 1; *bean,* sb. 8.

even that fish is going to catch up with him later, when he is described making love to May:

> He lulleth hire, he kisseth hire ful ofte—
> With thikke bristles of his beerd unsofte,
> Lik to the skin of houndfissh, sharpe as brere,
> For he was shave al newe in his manere. (E1823–6)

Old fish, ineptly razored, painfully embracing tender veal.

There is no need to labour the matter of Chaucer's careful portrayal of the uglier side of the central juxtaposition. This is made rank enough seriously to effect the quality, if not the quantity, of our laughter. Rather more subtle is his handling of that bright beast May. Initially she seems a sort of Galatea created in response to the fantasies of January; but despite the reckless assumption of the aged Pygmalion, the statue when it finally comes to life has no internal qualities to match its outward loveliness.[1] Of course, revelation of what May's qualities really are is postponed as long as possible. Meanwhile the Merchant associates with her—though he does not actually ascribe to her —such thoughts as the romanticist might think she ought to have: he manages to convey without an overt assertion her disgust with January's love-making; and when Damian becomes love-sick for her, the Merchant assures him in a rhetorical outburst that he can never attain her—'She wol alway saye nay'. But finally, on her visit to the squire, May allows him to thrust his letter into her hand, and she hides it in her bosom—her first genuine action in the poem. Thereafter the Merchant relates, with superbly bad taste, how, upon her return to January,

> She feined hire as that she moste goon
> Ther as ye woot that every wight hath neede,
> And whan she of this bille hath taken heede,
> She rente it al to cloutes at the laste,
> And in the privee softely it caste. (E1950–4)

In the word *softely* and the object with which it is juxtaposed is the climax of Chaucer's treatment of May, and the microcosm of his treatment of things throughout the poem as a whole. *Softly* had in Middle English as it still has a range of meanings

---

[1] The handling of May is discussed more fully below, pp. 50–3.

entirely appropriate to May's literal action, 'quietly, surrep-
titiously', and in this respect it is straightforwardly realistic.[1]
But *softly* also has, and cannot help having, another range of
meanings that associate it with warm weather, warm May,
tender, gentle, alluring womanhood, femininity at its most
romantically attractive; and thus the sense of the lines moves
backward and forward between May's beauty, May's deceit,
and the privy.

May is, however, alone within the poem in being allowed to
remain for any length of time unsullied, and the fact that everything else is sullied makes her descent seem inevitable even
while it is shocking. Indeed, if the narrative had turned suddenly,
at a point about halfway to the ending, from the beautiful to
the ugly, it might come closer to being the outrageous jest that
readers like Professor Bronson want it to be, for a really sudden
shock—like Thomas's gift to the Friar in the Summoner's Tale—
is likely to turn realism into fantasy. But the poem has been
infected with venom from the very beginning, a venom com-
pounded in part of a most cynical kind of realism. And this
venom is no mere overflow from the initial characterization of
the Merchant-narrator, but part of the tale's pigmentation. Let
us look for a moment at the passage that has been called Chaucer's most daring—or most rash—use of irony. The poem begins
with a quick sketch of the bachelor-lecher who in his old age
has determined to marry—'were it for holinesse or for dotage I
can nat saye':

> 'Noon other lif,' saide he, 'is worth a bene,
> For wedlok is so esy and so clene
> That in this world it is a Paradis.'
> Thus saide this olde knight that was so wis. (E1263–6)

After that last line, which is as near to a sneer as poetry can come,
the narrator intrudes to say:

> And certainly, as sooth as God is king,
> To take a wif, it is a glorious thing,
> And namely whan a man is old and hoor. (E1267–9)

These lines introduce a 126-line passage in which everything

---

[1] *OED*, *soft*, adj., notes that 'Many of the senses tend to involve or pass into each
other, esp. in poetic use'.

that might be said in favour of marriage gets itself said, and a good deal more. Readers have often observed that this passage has nothing in it to show that it is ironical beyond its context,[1] and some have even described it as a perfectly straightforward exposition of the medieval ideals of marriage. But Professor Bronson is right in noting that its sense, whatever its context, is absurd.[2] Indeed, it represents a kind of double distortion of reality: a rebuttal of antifeminism erected on the same bases as antifeminism. According to Jerome, who despite being a saint was not on this subject either clear-headed or fair-minded, the sole motive of a wife is to frustrate her husband. In the Merchant's panegyric, this simple formula is turned upside down with an equally simple-minded result: the sole motive of a wife is to assure her husband's comfort. Both opinions rest on the basic assumption that women were really created to be servile beasts, though according to one they reject their assigned role and according to the other they accept it gratefully. The masculine selfishness latent in the whole antifeminist tradition reaches its clearest expression in the Merchant's praise of matrimony: not 'he for God only, she for God in him', but he for himself, she for him. It is foolish though understandable to suppose, as January did, that May's beauty implies some special virtue, but it is simply absurd to suppose that wives will love their husbands just because they were kind enough to purchase them.

And not even this panegyric is allowed to bask uninterruptedly in the bright sunlight of its own vacuity: the shadow of bitterness falls here too, and in a rather surprising place. Following his source, which is either Chaucer's own *Melibeus* or its source, Albertano's endless *Book of Counsel*, the Merchant adduces the creation of Eve in order to establish for his hearers woman's usefulness to man:

> And herke why I saye nat this for nought
> That womman is for mannes help ywrought:
> The hye God, whan he hadde Adam maked,
> And sawgh him allone, bely-naked,
> God of his grete goodnesse saide than,

---

[1] The sentiments expressed in the passage are ascribed to January by the first line after its end, E1393: 'For which this Januarye ...'.

[2] *SP*, lviii (1961), 592–3.

> 'Lat us now make an help unto this man
> Lik to himself.' And than he made him Eve. (E1323–9)

I am unable to read this passage without feeling that in making Eve the Creator is motivated more by a kind of cynical pity than by love for what He has made. The clue to this feeling is that the narrator has substituted for God's statement, 'It is not good for a man to be alone', the action of God's looking at the poor naked thing and seeming to draw from Adam's appearance the conclusion that he had better have some help—there is no *imago Dei* here. 'And sawgh him allone, bely-naked.' Bely-naked is one of those phrases that offer pitfalls to the unwary. In my youth boys used to use it for the way they went swimming when there was no one to see; but it was evidently considered a vulgar phrase, for I don't believe we would have used it before our mothers, or not unscathed in any case; indeed, the word *belly* in any usage was so frowned upon that one still hears the euphemism *tummy* from the mouths of otherwise highly sophisticated speakers. But of course we have all been taught that those good old Anglo-Saxon words—and *belly* is from an Anglo-Saxon word meaning 'bag'—were commonly used in the Middle Ages, and that the vulgarity we associate with them is of relatively recent development. And surely this is sometimes so, but not so often as we think, and not, I think, in the present case. Chaucer only uses *belly* meaning 'stomach' three times in all his works.[1] One of these is in the brilliantly vulgar context of the Summoner's Tale, where it is referred to the highly gaseous churl who is to provide the gift that may be divided equally among thirteen friars. The other is in the Pardoner's sermon, a splendid example of what might be called homiletic shock-treatment, or Pauline hortatory vulgarity. For St Paul is, of course, the great original:

> O wombe, O bely, O stinking cod,
> Fulfilled of dong and of corrupcioun!
> At either ende of thee foul is the soun. (C534–6)

[1] Figures are based on the Tatlock-Kennedy *Concordance*. The other uses are at D2267 and C534. In the Parson's Tale (1350) *bely* means 'bellows', as Professor Norman Davis was kind enough to point out to me after I had originally misinterpreted it.

It seems a reasonable supposition that if Chaucer had not meant to have his narrator vulgarize the creation of Adam and Eve he would have chosen another term than *bely-naked*. 'And God saw Adam alone, belly-naked; and then of his great goodness he said, "Let us now make an help unto this man—like to himself". And then he made him Eve.' And Eve, another poor worm, is as like Adam as May turns out to be like January. It is a depressing thought.

This sour note, which sounds so often in the poem as to be characteristic of it, sounds again in the wedding of January and May, even more unharmoniously than it does in the Creation. Of course, one is fully aware that no marriage ceremony should be taking place between this ill-matched couple—that January is disobeying Cato's and Nature's precept that man should wed only his similitude. But the marriage ceremony itself is not responsible: it is not its fault that the bride and groom are unsuited, and it remains a 'ful greet sacrament'. Yet the narrator's 'mordant venom'—to borrow Professor Bronson's phrase again —sullies the ritual because he hates the participants:

> Forth comth the preest with stole aboute his nekke,
> And bad hire be lik Sarra and Rebekke
> In wisdom and in trouthe of mariage,
> And saide his orisons as is usage,
> And croucheth hem, and bad God sholde hem blesse,
> And made al siker ynough with holinesse. (E1703–08)

This passage—Mendelssohn on a flat piano—contains at least two dissonances that are worth examining. One is the repetition of the verb *bidden* (*bad*), used first in the sense 'command'—he commanded her to be like Sarah and Rebecca—and then in the sense 'pray'—he prayed that God would bless them. That is, 'pray' is the expected sense, but I can never read the passage without feeling that the second use of *bad* has been infected by the first, so that what the words really are saying is, 'And the priest told God to bless 'em'. The phrasing seems abruptly jussive. Indeed, my second translation, while idiomatic, is literally accurate. Moreover, there is some reason for making it, at least as a simultaneous alternate. In Chaucer's works the verb *bidden* occurs 124 times: 104 times it clearly means 'command', and only in twenty uses is the meaning 'pray' either requisite or probable. It occurs just six times with God as the object (*bidden God*), and in the other five the syntax is such as to make it clear that the bidder is making a request of God, not giving Him an order.[1] But here the syntax is bald: 'bad God sholde'. This construction seems to me to reflect the disgusted disillusion of the narrator, who here reduces, with a contempt bred of familiarity, Christian ritual to perfunctory hocus-pocus. The priest is seen as a kind of witch-doctor who presumably controls the Almighty much as Prospero controls Caliban. He dispenses holiness as if it were some sort of magic powder that he can scatter around in order to secure the marriage—an insecticide to ward off the flies of evil. But we know his magic isn't going to work. And that associations with primitive magic are what Chaucer had in mind as he wrote the lines is suggested by something else: when the priest makes the sign of the cross over the bride and groom, the verb used for the action is *crouchen*: 'And croucheth hem'. This Middle English word, common enough to have become part of the name of a whole order of friars, apparently had low associations for Chaucer: the only other time it occurs in his works is in the Miller's Tale, just before old John recites his ancient night-spell. Shaking Nicholas out of his assumed trance, John exclaims,

> I crouche thee from elves and fro wightes! (A3479)

Here, too, the background is one of primitive magic.

It is this recurrent action of derogating things-as-they-are, especially those things that we instinctively place value on, that imparts to the Merchant's Tale its large content of emotional energy. And when one's emotions are being constantly stirred up, one cannot read with detachment—cannot remain uninvolved. The Shipman's Tale, another study of opportunistic sexual behaviour marital and extramarital, produces an entirely

---

[1] See the Tatlock-Kennedy *Concordance* under *bade, bid, bidden, biddest, bidding*. I have made the greatest possible allowance for the potential meaning 'pray', but even so it is far less common than the meaning 'command'. The other occurrences with the direct object God are all in *TC*: I. 40 'biddeth God . . . To graunte'; III. 875 'I bidde God I . . . mote'; III. 1470 'I bidde God so yive'; IV. 738 'bad God on hire rewe'; V. 1007 'bidde I God . . . I may'. Only IV. 738 approaches the abruptness of the priest's prayer, and this is in a description of Criseide's hysterical grief.

different effect, because no grain of genuine emotion ever
scratches its smooth, glassy surface. Even the Reeve's Tale, a
vindictive story told by an angry man, evokes from all but the
most squeamish nothing but laughter: the fact that the Reeve
believes all millers to be thieves has not jaundiced his view of
life as a whole, and under his cool direction the fabliau-machine
works effortlessly to show that proud, thieving bullies get their
just deserts. But the Merchant's hard-earned conviction that
wives are inevitably and triumphantly deceitful and unfaithful
so infects his depiction of the world that the reader is made,
willy-nilly, to suffer some measure of pity and terror. It is easy
enough to laugh at futile, inarticulate wrath, as the pilgrims
laugh at the Pardoner when the Host's insult reduces him to
silence; but an articulate wrath that keeps wounding our
sensibilities necessarily involves us in itself. Detachment only
comes to the reader of the Merchant's Tale at the very end with
the culminating outrage, which is an incident of such high and
horrible fantasy that it disconnects us from our sense of reality.
Yet this detachment comes too late to alter the experience that
has gone before, and has, indeed, the paradoxical effect of enhancing its dark values. When May climbs the tree over January's
stooping back—tender youth over stooping age—we have to
surrender to laughter, but not without some of that sense of sadness we feel when what we have been emotionally involved
with moves beyond the point where we can any longer care.

In the meanwhile, between the wedding and the climax there
takes place a shift in the emotional balance of the two units in the
tale's central juxtaposition. Our natural sympathy for May,
evoked by her physical loveliness, and our natural disgust with
January reach their respective climaxes in the Merchant's
description of their wedding night. Professor Bronson tells us
that the mismating of youth and age 'was not the kind of problem that [Chaucer's] generation worried over',[1] but at least one
member of his generation, William Langland in Piers Plowman,
worried over it rather eloquently,[2] and it seems to me that

---

[1] SP, lviii (1961), 596.

[2] See the B-Text (ed. W. W. Skeat, London: EETS OS 38, 1869), ix. 154–76,
especially 160–1: 'It is an oncomely couple, bi cryst, as me þinketh, To ȝyuen a
ȝonge wenche to an olde feble' (probably olde should read ȝolde, i.e. '(sexually)
exhausted').

Chaucer took some trouble to make the reader of the Merchant's Tale worry over it when he quietly shifted the point of view of the narrative so that we see the wedding night through May's eyes rather than January's. But later, when May's female resourcefulness begins to work, some of the disgust we felt for January begins to spill over into our feeling for May: the eclipse is becoming total. And when January goes blind, some of the sympathy we felt for May is displaced and spills over into our feeling for him. Morally, of course, there is little to choose, nor has there been any real exchange of roles, for January is as bad as ever and May is merely revealing herself to be as bad as he. But moral judgment and emotion are not the same thing. We have been led by the Merchant's narrative, especially by his rhetoric, to make some emotional investment in the relationship, the juxtaposition, of January and May, and I for one find it hard immediately to liquidate the investment. The Merchant, by such devices as first defending May's concern for her honour in his rhetorical outburst against Damian, and then shortly afterwards congratulating her on her womanly resolve to be dishonest—

Lo, pitee renneth soone in gentil herte!— (E1986)

keeps the emotion sloshing back and forth between the weaker and the uglier vessel, frustrating hopes, spoiling values, and maintaining a state of nervousness from which only the most resolutely unflappable reader can free himself.

What seems to me the most triumphant stroke in the Merchant's rhetorical assault on our sensibilities occurs just after May has given Damian a key to the garden of delights and has 'egged' January into asking her to go with him there. The old lecher speaks his invitation:

> 'Ris up, my wif, my love, my lady free;
> The turtles vois is herd, my douve sweete;
> The winter is goon with alle his raines wete.
> Com forth now with thine yën columbin.
> How fairer been thy brestes than is win!
> The garden is enclosed al aboute:
> Com forth, my white spouse! out of doute,
> Thou hast me wounded in myn herte. O wif,

> No spot of thee ne knew I al my lif.
> Com forth and lat us taken oure disport—
> I chees thee for my wif and my confort.'
>   Swiche olde lewed wordes used he. (E2138–49)

'Such stupid old words he used.' This passage, with its devastating anticlimax, seems to me of itself a sufficient refutation of Bronson's belief 'that there is no intrinsic evidence' that Chaucer wrote the tale 'from a point of view predetermined by such a character' as the Merchant.[1] January's paraphrase of the Song of Solomon comes as close to poetry as the old man ever comes, and at least within hailing distance. Of course the passage has something of his inveterate lust, especially in the final couplet, 'lat us taken oure disport'. But if this were cut off and the rest printed, say, in one of Carleton Brown's collections of Middle English lyrics, I don't think it would shame its company or that any one who did not know would suspect from what context it came. It needs no dedicated patristic critic to point out that in the allegorical tradition the Song of Solomon was taken to represent Christ's love for the Church (or, alternatively, Christ's love for the human soul) and that the love of man and woman, expressed in marriage, was taken to be a mystical analogy of this divine love. Symbolically, the Song of Solomon represented the ideal of marriage. January sullies the symbol in his own way, but the Merchant with his gratuitous sneer wholly destroys its value as an ideal ever to be obtained by human beings. Previously he has dirtied the Creation of Adam and Eve and the rite of marriage, and now he has succeeded in dirtying the theological basis on which marriage was said to rest.

In so doing he has finally allowed the emotional and moral factors of the poem to unite. I dislike moralizing Chaucer's poetry, being persuaded that any work of art that presents an honest picture of existence as seen through any eyes, no matter how jaundiced, hateful, or even wicked the beholder may be, is moral enough of itself. But since I have categorically denied that the Merchant's Tale is primarily a merry jest, I suppose that I am forced to substitute something concrete for the laughter that I refuse to let take over the poem. It seems to me, then, that the Merchant's Tale was most carefully written to present the

[1] *SP*, lviii (1961), 596.

kind of world that can come into being if a man's approach to love and marriage is wholly mercantile and selfish—if he believes he can buy as a wife a domestic beast that will serve his every wish and, somehow, fulfil his most erotic fantasies. When the beast fails to be in its own right anything more than bestial, the purchaser may, like January, settle for an inner blindness which is more complete than physical blindness; or, like the Merchant, he may deliver himself to hatred—of the disappointing beast, of his own romantic dreams, of marriage, of himself. To read this tale without being disturbed by the force and truth of the Merchant's hatred seems to me impossible.

But I'm still feeling worried about my failure to laugh as loudly as others do. Is my sense of humour not robust enough? Perhaps. I prefer, however, to take refuge in the Merchant's own words in his description of the wedding feast of January and May:

> Whan tendre youthe hath wedded stouping age,
> Ther is swich mirthe that it may nat be writen.[1] (E1738-9)

---

[1] Despite my emphasis in this paper on the negative aspects of the Merchant's Tale, I do find certain positive values emerging at the seams of the story, without, as it were, the Merchant's knowledge. I tried to point some of these out in my discussion in Chaucer's Poetry, pp. 920–3, especially 923; but when I wrote I was without the benefit of the fine article by John Burrow, 'Irony in The Merchant's Tale', Anglia, lxxv (1957), 199–208.

4

THE MASCULINE NARRATOR
AND FOUR WOMEN OF STYLE

NOT LONG AGO an American Chaucerian harshly reprimanded those modern critics who talk about Chaucer as if he had a complicated or difficult style such as Donne's or Pope's. Chaucer, Professor Bronson asserts, was 'a poet who deliberately practised a style capable of being instantly followed by a moderately attentive ear, and who seems to have had a genuine liking for russet yeas and honest kersey noes'.[1] Therefore those who go digging in the poet's works with highly sophisticated tools, searching for buried subtleties, are guilty of the worst kind of critical vanity, which is to make what is really easy seem hard.

I have much sympathy for this point of view, despite the fact that a critical term I once used in connection with Chaucer seems to have provided one of the principal impulses for Professor Bronson's attack.[2] Chaucer does indeed have a simple, readily understandable style. Any poet who, near the beginning of a narrative about a trip to Canterbury, can expend eight laborious lines in order to inform us that, while he has time and space, before he goes any further in the story, he thinks it in accordance with reason to tell us *all* the condition of *each* of the people he met—according to the way it seemed to him, that is—and which they were, and of what degree, and also in what array that they were in, and finally announces that he will begin with a knight, and then climaxes this prospectus with the triumphant statement that there *was* a knight—well, such a poet is obviously so dedicated to the proposition that poetry should be understood

---

[1] B. H. Bronson, *In Search of Chaucer* (Toronto, 1960), p. 10.
[2] Such terms as *persona* in their application to Chaucer (see 'Chaucer the Pilgrim', reprinted above) are roundly castigated by Professor Bronson on pp. 25-9.

that he might almost be said to have cornered the market in russet and kersey. Nevertheless, I do not think that this is all that can be said of his style—that this is an end to it; if it were, I suspect that a few more sentences like the one I have just para- phrased (which is actually a self-parody) would have brought an end to most readers' acquaintance with his works, and that no Chaucer criticism would ever have grown to irritate Professor Bronson with its rank blossoms. In this paper I should like to investigate some passages in which a style that seems so simple and comprehensible is able to achieve effects that deserve a rather richer comparison than russet or kersey.

I shall concentrate on a single kind of effect—Chaucer's ability to describe things simultaneously from several distinct points of view while seeming to see them from only one point of view, and thus to show in all honesty the complexity of things while preserving the appearance of that stylistic simplicity which we feel to be so honest and trustworthy. The particular objects of his regard that I shall discuss are women—four attractive women, to be exact. I choose women because they are, obviously, the most complex topic that a man can try to deal with, a subject that no honest poet can hope to treat simply. An attractive woman requires even more complex handling, for she is likely to pro- voke in a man certain emotional responses that become, in any fiction, a part of her reality. That is why male narrators in literature so often fall in love with their heroines—to encourage the reader also to make an emotional investment from which he will expect, though not necessarily get, a return. Almost always with attractive women there is an element of deception—in literature, that is. A heroine fails to live up to the high ideals which a romantic male assumes to be a necessary corollary of her beauty, and thereby deceives him, or, more accurately, un- deceives him, which is worse. Or else her charm is such—'so absolute she seems, and in herself complete'—that his idea of what is right becomes unhinged, as happened to poor Adam. Or if she does live up to the male's romantic expectation, she may well cease to be a woman at all, and elude him by becoming a symbol or a cypher. In Chaucer's description of the four women I have chosen to talk about he has, with absolute honesty, brought it about that careful readers—those with attentive ears

—may perceive potentials that he himself seems not to see, preoccupied as he is with the ladies' outward beauty. The ladies are Emily, the symbolic heroine of the Knight's Tale; May, the downright deceitful heroine of the Merchant's Tale; Criseide, the disappointing heroine of *Troilus*; and the Prioress, a romance heroine masquerading as a nun.

Let us begin with Emily, who is from the human point of view one of the least interesting and hence least Chaucerian of Chaucer's heroines, though as an artistic creation she is splendid. Readers are so often disappointed by Emily because she has no character, and they are apt to blame Chaucer for not having given her any, failing to observe how very hard he has worked, in his simple-minded way, to see that she has none: for symbols such as Emily do not act, they merely are. We first meet her as she walks in the garden beneath the grim tower in which Palamon and Arcite are imprisoned:

> . . . It fil ones in a morwe of May
> That Emelye, that fairer was to seene
> Than is the lilye upon his stalke greene,
> And fressher than the May with flowres newe—
> For with the rose colour stroof hir hewe:
> I noot which was the fairer of hem two—
> Er it were day, as was hir wone to do,
> She was arisen and al redy dight,
> For May wol have no slogardye anight:
> The seson priketh every gentil herte,
> And maketh it out of his sleep to sterte,
> And saith, 'Aris and do thyn observaunce.'
> This maketh Emelye have remembraunce
> To doon honour to May and for to rise.
> Yclothed was she fresshe to devise;
> Hir yelow heer was broided in a tresse
> Bihinde hir bak a yerde long, I gesse,
> And in the gardin at the sonne upriste
> She walketh up and down, and as hire liste
> She gadreth flowres party white and rede
> To make a subtil gerland for hir hede,
> And as an angel hevenisshly she soong. (A1034-55)

Despite a measure of grammatical confusion which the modern editor is hard put to straighten out by dashes or parentheses, the style of the passage is simple enough, and the meaning is wholly clear: Emily is a pretty, long-haired blonde with a good complexion and an excellent singing voice. Yet while this information occupies four lines, the Knight has taken twenty-two to weave his tapestry. If we unravel the threads, we shall find that Emily is a good deal more—if a good deal less—than a woman. Not only is she like the May flowers that she is gathering, but she is also vying with them in beauty; and the fact is, of course, that she is herself a May flower which the warm sunrise of May wakes and causes to take its natural position in the garden of Spring. The poet seems to be trying to describe a woman, but he is actually showing us something of a rather different order. May, May, May, May; lily, stalk, flowers, garden, flowers, garland; green, rose, yellow, white, red; morning, day, sunrise: all the best of nature in the Spring, and all part of Emily, or rather, through the poet's intricate craft, of these things is Emily all compact. She becomes not only the embodiment of all pretty young girls in the Spring, but a proof that the Spring of pretty young girls is a permanent thing, and that May in their persons will always warm the masculine heart as May warms their hearts and sends them out among the flowers: 'Up rose the sun, and up rose Emily'. Like so many of Chaucer's narrators when they are describing attractive women, the aging Knight twice brings himself into the description as if he were himself trying to share more intimately the company of a creature not subject to time's decay—or, if it is, one that will always renew itself with each season and generation.

Of course the portrait lacks individuality. The whole Knight's Tale lacks individuality, for it is less concerned with real people than with the ideas and ideals by which people live in a real world, one which often seems devoid of purpose or significance. Emily is one of the ideas that make this world tolerable, and if she were given a personality, she would lose her symbolic significance as the goal toward which the better side of chivalry aspires. Within the tale she is scarcely permitted to act; she merely reacts to the incidents of the plot in a way which the Knight evidently considers ideally feminine, praying Theseus to spare the young knights' lives when they are found fighting in the wood, asking Diana to let her remain a maiden and then adapting herself becomingly to the prospect of marriage with Arcite, lamenting his untimely death, and finally living happily ever after with Palamon. She has no mind or character of her own, desiring only what most desires her, fulfilling in almost total passivity the symbolic function assigned to her in the Knight's initial description. Virtually untouched by the grim realities of the story, she gives recompense for them and makes the chivalric ideal come true, at least for Palamon and the reader. When Palamon first saw her he mistook her for a goddess; but I'm not sure that Arcite was not even more mistaken in supposing that she was a woman. She deceived them both, for she was only an idea, though one of more importance to the ideal of chivalry than a real woman could have been.

From Emily in her eternal May let us move to the heroine of the Merchant's Tale, whose deceptiveness begins with the fact that she bears the name of Emily's month. We first meet May in the night-time fantasies of the old lecher January, through whom we are to make whatever emotional investment we care to make in her:

> And when that he was in his bed ybrought,
> He portrayde in his herte and in his thought
> Hir fresshe beautee and hir age tendre,
> Hir middel smal, hir armes longe and sclendre,
> Hir wise governance, hir gentilesse,
> Hir wommanly bering and hir sadnesse. (E1599–1604)

With the easy self-deception of the romantic libertine, January first pictures to himself her physical charms, and then, as if by inference from these, her fine moral qualities: the boy's brain that accompanies his colt's tooth makes the Platonic assumption that May is all-of-a-piece, the passive exponent of her own loveliness, so that fresh beauty, tender age, small waist, and long slender arms necessarily imply wise behaviour, gentility, true femininity, and constancy. The reader himself is not permitted to see May until the wedding feast is being served:

> Mayus, that sit with so benigne a cheere
> Hire to biholde it seemed fairye—
> Queene Ester looked nevere with swich an yë
> On Assuer, so meeke a look hath she—

I may you nat devise al hir beautee,
But thus muche of hir beautee telle I may,
That she was lik the brighte morwe of May,
Fulfild of alle beautee and plesaunce. (E1742–9)

On first sight—or perhaps to only 'a moderately attentive ear'—
this passage seems not unlike the description of Emily: something about a beautiful woman and a May morning and a
narrator hard put to it to describe such beauty. But Chaucer in
his own devious way is playing quite honestly with us, for beneath the seemingly simple description of a romance heroine
there runs a disturbing undercurrent. The two specific qualities
of character that May's appearance suggests—benignity and
meekness—are initially pleasing, but as one dwells on them in
their emphatic isolation, they must appear to be too good to be
true, for they are the very qualities that a woman would need
in full measure in order to serve as bride to January, who is
evidently destined to have no such luck. The beauty of Emily
was unmixed with any traits of character, nor was she likened
to another woman. But May's is the meekness of Queen Esther,
whose charm was sufficient to accomplish the deaths of Haman,
his ten sons, and tens of thousands of other souls. Even that
haunting line, 'Hire to biholde it seemed faïrye', invokes a sense
of illusion—or delusion—and to the medieval reader probably
invoked a sense of something disquieting. Finally, the narrator
seems more than conventionally baffled in his attempt to describe May. May is the grammatical as well as the topical subject of the passage, but there is no verb to go with her: the
narrator is distracted into anacoluthon.[1] In similar grammatical
circumstances Emily had threatened to escape from the Knight,
but he caught her again by taking a by-path through the May
flowers, which he thus made part of her. The Merchant, however, breaks off as if wholly frustrated. The last four lines of an
eight-line passage of description consist of an acknowledgement
of his failure adequately to depict May's beauty. Instead of
depicting it, he uses the word 'beauty' itself in three of his four

[1] Robinson succeeds in avoiding the anacoluthon by putting a full stop after the
second line; he thus makes a main clause out of what I take to be a consecutive
clause dependent on a relative clause (that sit . . . cheere). Robinson's text would
presumably be translated, 'To behold May, who sits with so benign a look, seemed
magic'.

lines, and escapes from his cul-de-sac only by way of an arid double pun, rhyming the verb *may* with the month May in order to describe the woman May.

I should not wish further to infuriate Professor Bronson by suggesting that in this pun the verb *may*, while expressing grammatical potentiality, also suggests May's potentiality to be other than what her beauty might imply. Nevertheless, the effect of the whole passage is surely to suggest such potentiality, and the narrator's elaborate clumsiness must make a careful reader feel that there is something impenetrable about May's loveliness, a cool hardness that puts one off. One senses, moreover, no real enthusiasm in the description, almost, indeed, a kind of reluctance on the narrator's part to explore this woman's mystery. We may well suspect that what appears in her face to be the romance heroine's passivity is actually a latent potentiality for stealthy action. The suspicion that May has a shrewd mind of her own, though it is confirmed only late in the poem, is intermittently aroused in the reader during the intervening action. Thus while describing the morning after the bridal night the Merchant intrudes on the scene to say:

> But God woot what that May thoughte in hir herte
> Whan she him saw up sitting in his sherte,
> In his night-cappe and with his nekke lene—
> She praiseth nat his playing worth a bene. (E1851-4)

The last line is a splendid example of how in Chaucer the straight may become crooked. Strictly speaking, since the Merchant does not know what May thought—only God knows—her failure to praise January must be taken as negative narrative action: she did not speak praise of him, and yet, since she is not said to have spoken at all, she did not speak dispraise of him. On the other hand, the Merchant, by saying that she did not praise his playing *worth a bean*, that is, by seeming to use the very words with which May did not speak, has either contradicted his earlier disclaimer of knowledge or has foisted upon her his own thought. Of course the reader reading quickly what seem to be easily understood lines will not pause to make this awkward analysis, and will probably conclude that May's meekness and benignity have begun to give way when put to the test of January's love-making. But he will be wrong, for in his own devious way Chaucer is being careful to preserve, in letter if not in spirit, the fiction of the romance heroine's passivity until the last possible moment, while, of course, simultaneously suggesting to us that it is a fiction. The portrait of May is thus a curious combination of superficial honesty and subcutaneous deceit, taking its form from the woman it is describing.

Critics have sometimes noticed a similarity between May and Criseide, and I suppose they are right, although I resent their doing so because I remain as enchanted by Criseide as I am unenchanted by May. Yet Chaucer's descriptions of the two women do share something of the same technique, for since in both cases the women themselves will be ultimately revealed as untrue to what their beauty implies to the romantic beholder, in both cases the poet's honesty allows for this development from the very beginning. But Criseide, who has the larger function of destroying a truly romantic vision of life—not the falsely romantic, selfish one that May destroys—is handled with the most loving care, as befits so unusually charming a woman. In Book I the narrator makes three separate attempts to describe her, with the second and third perhaps suggesting his consciousness of having failed to do the job adequately in the first and second—although they also suggest the magnitude of his own emotional involvement. Here is the first description, which follows the summary of the Trojan war and of Calchas's treachery to his city and his daughter:

> Criseide was this lady name aright:
> As to my doom, in al Troyes citee
> Nas noon so fair, for passing every wight,
> So angelik was hir natif beautee,
> That lik a thing immortal seemed she,
> As dooth an hevenissh parfit creature
> That down were sent in scorning of nature. (TC 1.99–105)

One wonders whether the narrator may not, in this first attempt, have been working extraordinarily hard in order to counter the Biblical saying that nothing but bad fruit will come from a bad tree, a treacherous daughter from a treasonable father; for here the vocabulary is more ornate than in most of Chaucer's

5—s.o.c.

descriptions of women. Yet it is also highly conventional, and certainly not difficult to understand. Indeed, one might complain that the sense of the stanza lags behind its vocabulary: what the narrator has succeeded in saying is that Criseide was this lady's name aright (the word *aright* is one of those pedantic emphases by which Chaucer constantly reminds the reader that his style is easy),[1] and further, that in his opinion, there was none so fair in the whole city of Troy (and one wonders how he got to a Troy that was sacked several thousand years ago), because her natural beauty surpassed everyone's, being so angelic (or angel-like) that she seemed like an immortal thing (i.e., an angel), as does a heavenish perfect creature (i.e., an angel), of the kind that might be sent down in scorn of Nature (i.e., her natural beauty was so great that it was supernatural). In general, there seems to be no doubt about it: Criseide is as beautiful as an angel, and we romantic-minded men may expect that she will show a heroine's integrity: her role will be to reflect her beauty in her personality, naturally if rather inertly pleasing us. But we really know no more about her than if she were a complete mystery to the poet himself.

Seventy lines later, Criseide goes to the temple to attend the Feast of the Palladion, and the narrator tries to describe her again:

> Among thise othere folk was Criseida,
> In widwes habit blak, but nathelees,
> Right as oure firste lettre is now an *A*,
> In beautee first so stood she makelees:
> Hir goodly looking gladed al the prees.
> Nas nevere yit seen thing to been praised derre,
> Nor under cloude blak so bright a sterre,
>
> As was Criseide, as folk saide everichone
> That hire biheelden in hir blake weede. (1.169–77)

Notice how the narrator invokes the opinion of contemporary Trojans in support of what he is saying about Criseide. This is a device he often uses, sometimes rather irritably, when he seems to fear that readers, knowing the outcome, will not wholly

---

[1] Both Robinson and R. K. Root in *Chaucer's Troilus and Criseyde* (Princeton, 1926) prefer the even more pedantic variant *al right*.

share his enthusiasm for his heroine—not wholly believe in her seeming excellence. It is possible that the effect here will be the opposite of what seems intended—that some readers may be made to experience some doubt, not perhaps about Criseide's beauty, but about its implications. In any case, the narrator has not described a knowable woman: while she shines out from her black clothing like a star from behind a black cloud, Criseide has not yet left the skies to put on earthiness. The description continues:

> And yit she stood ful lowe and stille allone,
> Bihinden othere folk, in litel brede,
> And neigh the dore, ay under shames drede:
> Simple of attir and debonaire of cheere—

a timid, mild, meek angel obviously out of place in the ambiguous position on earth she has been left in by her mortal father. All this is highly conventional, highly romantic in the easiest sense of the word: a fair damsel in distress. But the stanza ends:

> ... and debonaire of cheere,
> With ful assured looking and manere.

So unexpected is this last line that one is tempted to split it off from Criseide and apply it to the still confident Troilus, who appears as the subject of the next sentence, leading his companions up and down in the temple and making fun of love. Such a division would be grammatically and textually possible, but it would be wrong. For Criseide has finally made the trip from heaven to earth, almost without the narrator's having noticed it: standing full lowly, still, alone, behind other folk, a little apart, near the door, under shame's dread, simple of attire, mild of face—with look and manner full assured. If ever a line cried for expatiation, it is this one, but the narrator, as if caught up by the narrative action, turns straight to Troilus. Yet the unexpected juxtaposition lingers in the mind for a moment, at once charming and remotely disquieting, for we do not understand how so conventionally timid a creature comes to possess such sudden self-assurance. By learning more about Criseide we know less: detail increases her mystery

not our knowledge of her. But if we hurry on with the narrator we will soon forget any uneasiness that may have arisen
in us, submerging it in the delight we receive from the whole
portrait.

Ninety-eight lines later there occurs the third portrait of Criseide. Having finally accepted the fact that she is a woman, the
narrator describes her as such:

> She nas nat with the leeste of hir stature,
> But alle hir limes so wel answeringe
> Weren to wommanhood, that creature
> Was nevere lasse mannish in seeminge;
> And eek the pure wise of hir mevinge
> Shewed wel that men mighte in hir gesse
> Honour, estaat, and wommanly noblesse. (I.281–7)

If one reads the stanza quickly, one is almost certain to get the
impression that what Chaucer has said is that Criseide's appearance proved that she had admirable qualities of character, which
any one who looked at her could see. But if one reads carefully,
one will find that the poet has proceeded with remarkable
caution, and has, indeed, told us nothing more about Criseide
than that, being a very beautiful woman, she was attractive to
men. She was not the smallest of women (which does not mean
that she was the tallest, or even that she was tall), but all her
limbs so well answered to womanhood that no creature could
have seemed less masculine—that is, she looked entirely female.
And the very way she moved showed well that men might guess
there to be in her honour, estate, and womanly noblesse. This
last sentence is another fine example of how to achieve honesty
by deceit: one can hardly help reading it to mean that the way
she moved proved that she had womanly noblesse; but in fact
it means that the way she moved looked so well that, as a result,
men might guess she had it. In other words, the readily understandable sense is not the same as the grammatical sense.
Chaucer the poet has further enhanced Criseide's charm, but
Chaucer the grammarian has been careful to draw no inferences
from it. *Caveat spectator*—in this case, both Troilus and the romantic reader.

Once again the description is amplified, and modified, by the
narrative action. The next stanza continues:

To Troilus right wonder wel withalle
Gan for to like hir meving and hir cheere,
Which somdeel deinous was, for she leet falle
Hir look a lite aside in swich manere
Ascances, 'What, may I nat stonden here?'
And after that hir looking gan she lighte,
That nevere thoughte him seen so good a sighte.

Once again that tantalizing self-assurance, momentarily dis-quieting, ultimately enhancing her mystery and charm. On most masculine readers, as on Troilus and the narrator, the effect of this lovely meek woman whose look can be a challenge will be devastating. We will not worry about how she goes about the business of 'lighting her looking', since such a woman can obviously do anything to please. So charmed are we that we readily forget that we still know nothing about her except that she is charming.

It would be a gross oversimplification to say that the rest of the poem consists of a gradual discovery on everyone's part that Criseide is, while altogether charming, little else, 'matter too soft a lasting mark to bear'. But it would not be too misleading to say that it is one of the qualities that the romanticist imputes to her on first sight that helps betray her: her passivity, which insures that she will behave in such a way as to please the on-looker, and desire what most desires her. But the onlooker must be physically present to look on her and to desire her: separated from Troilus, she is desirable in Diomede's eyes, to whom she resolves that she 'wol be trewe'. It is interesting that the narra-tor, ultimately forced to face the actuality of Criseide's infidelity to Troilus, tries to understand it by looking upon her once more, in a final description of her. This occurs in the well-known passage in Book V that has as its source the earliest of all descrip-tions of Criseide, the one given in Dares of Crete (though Chaucer knew it through Joseph of Exeter). In Chaucer's poem, Diomede has been urging himself on Criseide in the Greek camp, hardly believing that even his experienced technique will win her. The narrator breaks off the story for a moment to describe Diomede, and then moves on to Criseide:

Criseide mene was of hir stature,
Therto of shap, of face, and eek of cheere,

> Ther mighte been no fairer creature;
> And ofte times this was hir manere:
> To goon ytressed with hir heres clere
> Down by hir coler at hir bak bihinde,
> Which with a threed of gold she wolde binde;
>
> And, save hir browes joineden yfere,
> Ther nas no lak in ought I can espyen. (v.806–14)

While there are a number of echoes of the descriptions in Book I, the romantic excitement has gone, replaced by a kind of puzzled melancholy, as though the narrator were painfully going over what he had said before in order to find out what had gone wrong. Reviewing the topic, he picks up petty details not mentioned before: her medium stature, which earlier had been vaguely described as not the smallest; a not very remarkable coiffure, which occupies four lines; joined eyebrows, the only fault he can see—notice the curious nostalgia that arises from his still being able to see a woman whom he had never known and who had, indeed, died thousands of years before he was born. And once again he reinforces his own opinion with the testimony of others:

> But for to speken of hir yën clere,
> Lo, trewely, they writen that hire sien
> That Paradis stood formed in hir yën;
> And with hir riche beautee everemore
> Stroof love in hire ay which of hem was more.

These lines show a sudden powerful surge back toward the initial vision that has been frustrated—the vision of Paradise in a woman's eyes, a land of lush beauty and of high passion. Like the old men on the walls of Troy watching Helen pass, the narrator is suddenly requickened, and he seems on the point of trying to restore to the poem the rich romantic values it once had. But reillusionment is not possible, and he continues with his sad examination of the facts:

> She sobre was, eek simple and wis withal,
> The beste ynorisshed eek that mighte be,
> And goodly of hir speeche in general;
> Charitable, estaatlich, lusty, free,
> Ne nevere mo ne lakked hire pitee:

Tendre-herted, sliding of corage—
But trewely I can nat telle hir age.

The style of this stanza is wholly different from anything we have encountered before in the ground covered by this paper. It is, indeed, closer to the style of the portraits in the General Prologue to the *Canterbury Tales*, and Chaucer is in a very real sense presenting us with a person we have hardly known before: we thought we knew her, but we didn't. Like some of the portraits in the General Prologue the passage concludes with an anticlimax—indeed, a double anticlimax. After all those admirable attributes, so natural to a woman with a kind, tender, and responsive heart, the simple fact that Criseide was 'sliding of corage', that her heart was unstable, comes as the unemphatic explanation of everything that has occurred in the sad dénouement of the poem—a highly simplified explanation, to be sure, but one whose logical force is irresistible; in its limited way, it is true and honest. Yet Chaucer here, as often elsewhere, gives an explanation for his poem that will satisfy our reasoning faculties because of its perfect suitability to the facts of the plot, but will leave our imaginations floundering in anticlimax, with most of our questions unanswered. It is true that we have never known Criseide; but most readers will prefer to continue not to know her rather than accept simple instability of heart as the key that unlocks her mystery. And the narrator himself finishes the portrait by invoking the unknown in his last line and second anticlimax: for 'trewely' he 'can nat telle hir age'. All that is certain is that this immortal-seeming creature was most subject to time and to change, and that her mutability is indeed the sole reason for her immortality.

From Criseide to the Prioress is an easy transition suggested by the similarity of phrases in the last stanza quoted to phrases in the portrait of the Prioress.[1] But the narrator of *Troilus* had described a heroine of romance whose conventional romance qualities did not enable her to endure the tests imposed by the real world. The narrator of the General Prologue, on the other hand, is trying to describe a nun who, in the real world, is better

[1] See, e.g., A. C. Cawley, 'A Note on Chaucer's Prioress and Criseyde', *MLR*, xliii (1948), 74–7.

fitted to be a romance heroine. And even more than in *Troilus*, the tension (to use a somewhat weary critical term) between what is and what is expected exists primarily in the mind of the beholder. The portrait of the Prioress is the fourth of the series in the General Prologue, following those of Knight, Squire, and Yeoman. From the time the Knight first began to ride out, he loved chivalry—that is, from the time that he first became a knight he loved being a knight—and all his traits of character are interchangeable with those of an ideal knight. So it is also, on a less exalted scale, with the Squire and the Yeoman. After three such perfect examples of congruency between the person described and his profession, both the reader and the narrator may well expect more of the same. And the description starts promisingly enough:

> Ther was also a Nonne, a Prioresse— (A118)

a statement that names the lady's profession twice, raising her nunliness to a higher mathematical power, as it were. One would not be surprised if the next line were to read:

> Devout she was, and loved holinesse—

if, that is, the portrait had begun on the odd line. But the portrait begins on the even line, and it is the next line that is odd:

> That of hir smiling was ful simple and coy.

It is easy to ignore how very odd this line is, for it follows with such plausible simplicity upon its predecessor, as if the first thing any one would want to know about a nun would naturally be the quality of her smiling—and after that, of course, the manner of her swearing:

> Hir gretteste ooth was but by sainte Loy.

And so the portrait continues, as if the narrator were happy that for once in his life he has met a real-life romance heroine. But the old deception is inevitably present because, of course, she is a nun. Yet this incongruity is less a part of her consciousness than of the narrator's—until that is, he succeeds in exorcising it. Mindful of her profession, he manages to work in a reference to the divine service, if only to emphasize the aesthetic aspects of her rendition of it. But thereafter, charmed by the woman, he gets down to the really basic stuff of her table manners, and after five lines of graceful eating achieves what is apparently a terminal generalization on this aspect of the Prioress:

> In curteisye was set ful muchel hir lest.

But the Lord Chesterfield in him has been too strongly stimulated by her dining-table elegance, and he turns from generalization back to specifics in order to make it clear that she drank every bit as daintily as she ate. Only then is he free once more to describe her in general terms, using some of the same ones that we have seen applied to Criseide. Then, in the twenty-fifth line of a forty-five line portrait, the awareness that he is talking about a nun returns to halt his descriptive progress with a sudden jerk:

> But, for to speken of hir conscience,
> She was so charitable and so pitous—.

But if he had thought to get her back to the convent's chapel-door with the high-Christian ideas of conscience, charity, and pity, he was mistaken, for she has gone off on her own way again, feeling sorry for mice and spoiling small dogs. And so, with one last defiant assertion that at once affirms and dismisses her religious side,

> And al was conscience and tendre herte,

he turns, with obvious relief, to what both she and he are more interested in, her perfectly delightful appearance. *Amor vincit omnia.*

In discussing these portraits of four women I have tried to show some of the ways in which Chaucer can create complexity with his basically simple style—or rather, with a style that might better be called deceptively simple. In all four women there is an element of deception built into their descriptions. Emily is presumably a woman, but emerges from her description as the symbol of what may make the ideal of chivalry worthwhile. May seems the lovely meek victim of senile lust, but her potentiality for relieving her predicament in the most ruthless way is implicit in her description. Criseide, most charming of women, is candidly described as an ideal heroine of romance whose mystery the reader is encouraged, but not forced, to explore in search of qualities as fair as her own person is, only to find that in the end the mystery remains, and the qualities are, at best, insufficient. And finally the Prioress, whom the narrator tries to describe as a religious but ends up by describing, in all delighted honesty, as a romance heroine, thereby accomplishing, without using one satiric word, a double satire, on himself as a man as well as on her as a nun.

Although the Prioress herself is not really a complex woman, her portrait is surely one of the most complex brief portraits in English literature. Moreover, it concludes with a touch that seems to me representative of Chaucerian simplicity at its most diabolical. You will recall that after the narrator has finished his actual description, he adds the couplet,

> Another Nonne with hire hadde she
> That was hir chapelaine, and preestes three. (A163–4)

Stylistically speaking, there isn't a simpler sentence in Chaucer, a plain statement of plain fact. Yet although the couplet appears in all complete manuscripts—and the second line is one of those great rarities in the *Canterbury Tales*, a line with no manuscript variations—scholars as far back as Tyrwhitt have often questioned the authenticity of those three priests.[1] Perhaps the principal stated objection to them is that they contradict another plain statement of fact, that there were twenty-nine pilgrims, for three priests would make at least thirty-one; and of course two of them never show up again in the *Canterbury Tales*. But one suspects that scholarly doubt about the priests is not unin-fluenced by a certain gentlemanly impulse to save the Prioress's reputation: and one can point out, as Manly did, that the Con-vent of St Leonard's in Stratford-atte-Bowe (to which scholars, repairing Chaucer's omission, have assigned her) was too small

---

[1] Thomas Tyrwhitt, *The Canterbury Tales of Chaucer* (London, 1775–8), i, 'Intro-ductory Discourse'. See also J. M. Manly ed., *Canterbury Tales* (New York, 1928), pp. 507–8; Manly-Rickert, ii, 95, and iii, 422–3; Robinson, p. 655; and A. C. Baugh, ed. *Chaucer's Major Poetry* (New York, 1963), p. 241.

to allow its Prioress three priests on her journeyings.[1] Thus the majority of Chaucer's recent editors have agreed in assigning the priests to a curious limbo: they appear clearly in the text, but are rendered non-existent by the notes.[2] Now you see them, now you don't. In order to kill off Partridge, Swift turned both himself and Partridge into fictions; but one feels that the scholars, overcome by the charming verisimilitude of the portrait of the Prioress, have in their own real persons turned her fictional priests into real priests in order to prove that they have no fictional existence.

Fortunately there have been those who uphold the right of the three priests to remain in the text, notably Professors Sherbo and Hamilton.[3] And Mrs Hamilton has re-emphasized Skeat's important point that Chaucer's nine-and-twenty is not the exact number it is often taken to be.[4] Chaucer did, indeed, avoid using thirty, a round number which generally means in Middle and Modern English *about* thirty; but having chosen the utterly specific number twenty-nine, Chaucer then made it unspecific again by writing 'wel nine and twenty', which means 'fully' or 'at least' but not 'exactly' twenty-nine. This is a microcosm of his style: he gets credit for being an honest, straightforward, clear-headed narrator, while allowing himself a dishonest leeway of one, or two, or three: an honest russet number is made dishonest by its kersey modifier.

So much for Chaucer's reputation for honest dealing. But what about the lady's? Should the only fictional Prioress that St Leonard's ever enjoyed be going to Canterbury in the company of three priests? Surely not. Yet, like all the attractive women we have been examining, she is a romance heroine, and a most attractive one at that; and, as we have seen, the reaction of men to a romance heroine is a part of her character. I'm afraid that the three priests are a part of the Prioress's character, and while

---

[1] See Manly's 1928 edition, p. 508.

[2] An exception is Robert A. Pratt, ed., *Selections from the Tales of Canterbury and Short Poems* (Boston, 1966) who omits the words 'and preestes three' from A164, leaving the line incomplete.

[3] Arthur Sherbo, 'Chaucer's Nun's Priest Again', *PMLA*, lxiv (1949), 236–46; Marie P. Hamilton, 'The Convent of Chaucer's Prioress and Her Priests', *Philologica: The Malone Anniversary Studies*, ed. T. A. Kirby and H. B. Woolf (Baltimore, 1949), pp. 179–90.

[4] *Philologica*, p. 182; W. W. Skeat's multivolumed Oxford *Chaucer* (1894), v, 19.

it may be courteous of scholars to try to relieve her of moral responsibility for them, it is untrue to that simple, trustworthy narrator, Geoffrey Chaucer. I'm sure he enjoyed awarding his creation such company, and I hope she is properly grateful to her creator. In any case, I am happy to think that even after five and a half centuries the Prioress is continuing her journey to Canterbury in the company of her three priests, probably making a fool of herself, but surely capable, like other attractive women, of making even bigger fools of us male critics.

5

CRISEIDE AND HER NARRATOR

WHEN IN THE second book of *Troilus* Pandarus has finally ended
the interview in which he has told Criseide that Troilus loves
her, she goes to her room and sits down in order to think carefully about her situation. But before she has been able to do so
for much more than a stanza, she hears some one cry from the
street that Troilus is about to ride by, fresh from a victorious
skirmish with the Greeks. Criseide looks out at him from her
window, and is so stirred by his manly appearance that she asks
herself the famous question, 'Who yaf me drinke?' and 'of hir
owene thought' waxes 'al reed'. Ashamed, she pulls her head
in; and a stanza is expended telling us how she then went over
his excellent qualities in her mind, and liked him because of
them, but liked him mostly because his distress was all for her.
At this point the narrator interrupts his own account of her
action to comment on it:

> Now mighte som envious jangle thus:
> 'This was a sodein love. How mighte it be
> That she so lightly loved Troilus,
> Right for the firste sighte? Ye, pardee!'
> Now who so saith so, mote he nevere ythee,
> For every thing a ginning hath it neede
> Er al be wrought, withouten any drede. (II.666-72)

I have elsewhere suggested my wonder about the number of
first readers of the poem who have been worrying up to this
point about the rapidity with which Criseide's emotions are
turning toward Troilus.[1] It may be that some have felt that she
is moving a little more quickly than is wholly becoming to
widowly modesty; others, however, may well feel that she is
behaving in a perfectly natural way—that a woman with no

---

[1] *Chaucer's Poetry*, pp. 969-70.

domestic ties who has just learned that a handsome and eminent young man is desperately in love with her has every right to be curious about him and at least to speculate on how it would feel to love him. Thus it is possible to read the passage I have summarized as describing no more than an honest female reaction involving her in no necessary consequences, for Criseide's behaviour so far commits her to nothing. But of course every one is aware of the basic fact on which the poem rests— that Criseide did come to love Troilus and that she forsook him before she died, and this awareness will inevitably encourage some readers to examine every action she performs for signs of instability, or light-mindedness, or insincerity. It is evidently these readers that the narrator is castigating in the stanza I have just quoted, though he rebukes them, characteristically, not for suspiciousness but for envy ('ill-will'). But the unfortunate thing about his comment is that, while presumably suppressing the suspicions of a minority, he has implanted these very suspicions in the minds of all his readers. People who had never thought that there was any formal law governing the rate of speed at which a woman should fall in love may suddenly start believing there is one, and go looking in Andreas Capellanus to find out whether Criseide has exceeded the limit. Or they may reread Chaucer's own account of Criseide's behaviour in search of information which will help them define her rate of speed, and thus perhaps they will interpret certain ambiguities in the passage unfavourably.[1] Nor is the narrator's comment quite satisfactory, for what his stanza is apt to leave in one's mind is not the sententiously fuzzy saying that everything has a beginning before it's done, but the strong statement that is being denied: 'This was a sodein love'.

Furthermore, a second stanza that the narrator adds for reinforcement, a wordy attempt to differentiate between initial

---

[1] Perhaps 'ambiguity' is not quite the right word for a meaning which is so lightly suggested as to be almost imperceptible to one reading at normal speed and in the expectation that the sense will not deviate from a certain norm of decorum. But Criseide's blush in II.652 is probably partly explained by the fact that upon seeing Troilus ride by on his return from battle she observed that 'bothe he hadde a body and a might To doon that thing' (633–4) and that he was 'weeldy' (636). The verb weelden has, inevitably, a common sexual sense in Middle English, and 'that thing' seems a probable euphemism.

liking and fully committed loving, fails because of its own laborious precision, which inadvertently emphasizes the fact that liking and loving, while differing in intensity, are stages in the same general process, and are not necessarily separated by a time interval of any large duration. For all the narrator's efforts to suggest the contrary—indeed, because of them—it may well seem to hitherto unsuspicious readers that Criseide liked Troilus on May fourth and loved him on May fifth. And when, in a third stanza, the narrator, himself eagerly looking forward to the love affair, informs us that Venus was at the time in her seventh house and hence disposed to help Troilus, and that anyhow she was not entirely his foe in his nativity, and hence

God woot that wel the sonner spedde he— (II.686)

well, after all this, one can only conclude that it took either a very long short time or a very short long time for Criseide's love to blossom. If there was any initial confusion in the reader's mind about the whole matter, the narrator has succeeded in much confounding it.

When Kittredge likened *Troilus* to a psychological novel, he undoubtedly did the poem a service by calling attention to the extraordinary psychological insight it often manifests. But he did the poem a disservice by seeming to suggest—inadvertently, I believe—that if we study its characters steadily we shall find that they operate according to recognizable patterns of be-haviour, responding logically to the stresses that the situation imposes on them. This may be true of some of Chaucer's characters—perhaps of the Wife of Bath, who is presented from only one point of view, her own, and without editorial com-ment from her creator. But I am certain that the psychological approach inevitably fails with Criseide, although she seems to me to represent Chaucer's supreme achievement in the creation of human character. The difficulty with Criseide, as I hope the passage I have discussed from Book II will have suggested, is that she is not seen from any consistently detached, objective point of view: she is seen almost wholly from the point of view of a narrator who is so terribly anxious to have us see only the best in her, and not to see the worst even when it is staring both us and him in the face, that when he is afraid we will see something he doesn't want us to see, he plunges in to muddy up the water so that we can't see anything clearly.[1] Indeed, in order to understand Criseide properly we should first have to send the narrator to a psychoanalyst for a long series of treatments and then ask him to rewrite the poem on the basis of his own increased self-knowledge. It is with the wildly emotional attitude of the narrator of the poem and what it does to shape our idea of Criseide—and what Chaucer does through the narrator to reshape it—that I shall deal here.

The most obvious, and all-important, fact about the narrator is that he loves Criseide; not as a lover, though he shares Troilus's boyish idolatry of her, but rather he loves her with something of the avuncular sentimentality that Dickens lavishes on several of his more intolerable heroines. For the narrator, Criseide can do no wrong, not even fall in love in a way some one might not approve, as we have just seen. Yet the historical fact is that Criseide did do wrong and did it in a way that may well cause readers to hate her. While this fact is stated clearly enough at the beginning of the poem, it is never mentioned again in the first three books, a period during which the narrator's love is permitted triumphantly to express itself as he completes the portrait of a most wonderfully attractive and lovable woman. Only a very few times in this part of the poem is any shadow of uneasiness allowed to fall across the sunlit pages of the love story: we have seen one of the times when, if no actual shadow fell, the brightness did momentarily threaten to diminish—as a result, curiously enough, of the narrator's deep desire that the brightness should not be impaired. But in the fourth book, when the sun nears the horizon, and in the fifth book, when it sinks below it, there is no way to prevent the encroachment of shadows. Yet the narrator does his best to maintain his belief that so lovely a woman as Criseide could do no wrong. And it is here that Chaucer interferes with the work of his narrator—whom he has created not quite in his own image—in order to add to his poem that complexity of vision that he shares with only very few other English poets, and those the greatest. At some of the moments when his narrator is striving most laboriously to palliate Cri-

[1] The general matter of the narrator's relation to Criseide is discussed more fully above, pp. 53–9.

seide's behaviour, Chaucer, standing behind him, jogs his elbow, causing him to fall into verbal imprecision, or into anticlimax, or making his rhetoric deficient, or making it redundant— generally doing these things in such a way that the reader will be encouraged almost insensibly to see Criseide in a light quite different from the one that the narrator is so earnestly trying to place her in. I began this paper with an example of this kind of rhetorical failure from Book II, though at that early point in the story the effect is probably to leave the reader only puzzled, not really worried. In the last two books, however, the effects are more sinister, as what might be called the logic of fact begins to oppose the logic of love, though without ever being able wholly to countervail it. Let us examine some of these passages in order to see how they contribute to our imaginative perception of Criseide.

The third book of the poem ends with the statement that Troilus is with Criseide, 'his owene herte sweete', and the fourth book begins with an adversative conjunction—that *but* whose clause is always, in life as in literature, spoiling the high hopes of its grammatical predecessor:

> But al too litel, wailaway the while,
> Lasteth swich joye, ythanked be Fortune. (IV.1–2)

Like any good medieval man, the narrator sets out to blame what is to come on Fortune, at whom he rails, for a stanza and more, in good set terms, apparently trying to postpone for as long as he can the fact—unmentioned for more than 4600 lines—that regardless of the part played by Fortune, it was Criseide who was the immediate cause of Troilus's unhappiness. Indeed, his phrasing is unlucky, for when he says that Fortune cast Troilus

> ... clene out of his lady grace,
> And on hir wheel she sette up Diomede,

the distinction between the two women, Fortune and Criseide, tends to blur, and the goddess's fickleness rubs off on the mortal lady. In the next lines the narrator finally does bring himself to face directly the fact of Criseide's role in the history:

> And now my penne, allas, with which I write,
> Quaketh for drede of that I moste endite.
>
> For how Criseide Troilus forsook— (IV.13–15)

a manful stroke of a quaking pen, restating unambiguously for
the second and last time the basic fact on which the whole action
depends. But for the narrator, the fact is too bald, and he hurries
to soften its effect:

> Or at the leeste how that she was unkinde
> Moot hennesforth been matere of my book,
> As writen folk thurgh which it is in minde. (16–18)

Euphemism is successful only when it stands in the place of a
strong statement; when it follows the strong statement that it
purports to replace, as it does here, it accomplishes no more
than an anticlimax. Criseide's forsaking of Troilus is emphasized,
rather than palliated, by the narrator's attempt to minimize
it. And of course he has no historical authority for his suggestion
that she was merely unkind. Therefore he explores a new
possibility:

> Allas that they sholde evere cause finde
> To speke hire harm—and if they on hire lie,
> Ywis, hemself sholde han the vilainye. (19–21)

But even the most soft-hearted of historians could hardly argue
that the only authorities for Criseide's existence were telling
lies about the act of infidelity which was almost the only reason
that her existence was recorded. There is only one version of the
story of her infidelity, and at this point the narrator would like
to get through it quickly, for he calls on the furies and Mars to
help him conclude in this same fourth book. Yet it takes him,
of course, two long books to complete the story. Perhaps his
desire for a quick release from a deteriorating situation came to
be balanced in his mind by the hope that he might somehow do
something to excuse his lady.

When the news that her exchange for Antenor has been ar-
ranged is brought to Criseide, she inwardly curses the bearer,
but because she fears to face the possibility that the report is
true, she dares ask no one for clarification—

> As she that hadde hir herte and al hir minde
> On Troilus yset so wonder faste,
> That al this world ne mighte hir love unbinde,
> Ne Troilus out of hir herte caste. (673–6)

For those of us who love Criseide these lines are unambiguous enough: her heart and mind were so firmly fixed on Troilus that the whole world could not unbind her love for him. But the form of expression is a little strange. The sentence begins as if it were introducing a full-blown simile—'as she' or 'like a woman' that had her heart, etc.—but the simile turns out to be merely a direct description of Criseide herself. I am aware that I am treading on very slippery ground here, but I can't help feeling a slight uneasiness at the abrupt frustration of my expectation of a simile. A simile, of course, likens two things that are essentially dissimilar, and the mind takes note of the dissimilarity while registering the likeness. Here the expectation of a simile causes one to assume that Criseide will be likened to something from which she is essentially different and which possesses a greater imaginative immediacy than she, and when it turns out that she is only like herself one may feel that she is rather less than one thought. All but the very simplest uses of *as* to express equivalence cause a distancing between the things compared: 'He spoke as one who had suffered' is not as direct or unambiguous a statement as 'One could tell from his speech that he had suffered'. But in the last two books of *Troilus* Chaucer rarely if ever permits the narrator to say in his own person, and in so many words, that Criseide loved Troilus. There is always a distancing device, if only one so seemingly negligible as the little *as*. Yet the cumulative effect of such devices may well weaken one's confidence that what is said to be real is real.

I do not want to suggest that this single, tiny, isolated point— this butterfly that I am breaking so cruelly on the wheel of my criticism—should be understood as an indisputable judgment upon Criseide, or that we should straightway start looking at her from the point of view of Shakespeare's Thersites. Far from it: the narrator is himself in one of his tenderest moods as far as the lady is concerned, and we should respect his feelings. I am suggesting, however, that Chaucer has allowed the narrator's rhetoric to fall a little short of our expectations at a rather crucial moment: the reminder that Criseide is soon to prove unfaithful is still very fresh in our minds, and the inferences we may draw from this foreknowledge are, like pigeons after a recent alarm, still on the wing, searching for resting places. Using different terms, one might say that the narrator's phrasing subliminally awakens the reader's sense of distrust, and that this distrust naturally alights upon Criseide. The mind tends to search among things past for the potentialities that are being realized in things present, and given foreknowledge will search in the present for signs of things that are to be realized in the future. I think that in this passage we are being encouraged to search, though I do not think we are invited to find.

Certainly in the following scenes the genuineness of Criseide's grief is not open to question, for it is described at great length and with what is—for this narrator—a surprising objectivity. He does not intrude to comment on or even to try further to enhance her sorrow until after the soliloquy in which she resolves to die—by starvation, since weapons frighten her—and to wear black until she dies. Then the rhetoric bursts forth:

> How mighte it evere yred been or ysonge,
> The plainte that she made in hir distresse—
> I noot; but as for me, my litel tonge,
> If I descriven wolde hir hevinesse,
> It sholde make hir sorwe seeme lesse
> Than that it was, and childisshly deface
> Hir heigh complainte, and therfore ich it pace. (799–805)

On the surface there is no compelling reason to suspect the sincerity of this disclaimer—conventional enough in form—of the narrator's ability to repeat Criseide's complaint, despite its position following a forty-two-line rehearsal of her complaint. But the facts of history—still, in this case, future history—make it seem at least a tactless disclaimer. One simply ought not to frame words that invoke a discrepancy between what Criseide's sorrow seems to be and what it is, no matter how emphatically the words themselves deny a real discrepancy. We are so acutely aware that a time will come when her sorrow will be consoled that we are apt to transmute the narrator's fear of failing to do justice to her feeling into a failure on her part genuinely to feel. Furthermore, there is another breach of tact in the stanza: its last words, 'and therfore ich it pace', while presumably expressing the narrator's disgust with his own incompetence, are not entirely devoid of that impatience with which Chaucer's narrators dismiss topics that are beginning to bore them in favour of something more interesting—and, as a matter of fact, in the next line the narrator moves to the topic of Pandarus. It would be too much to say that the passage childishly defaces a subject that its overt purpose is to avoid childishly defacing, but as a rhetorical enhancement of Criseide's grief it leaves something to be desired. But let me emphasize that if, as lawyers, we were to call Chaucer into court we could never convict him of having brought Criseide's sincerity into question; on the other hand, as readers we may tend to feel that she bears some responsibility for having become the victim of the narrator's incompetence.

The narrator does not let himself appear in the woefully pathetic scene between Criseide and her uncle, and he intrudes again only very late in the equally pathetic scene between Troilus and Criseide during their last night together. After Criseide has finished her long enumeration of all the schemes she has in mind for getting back to Troy, the narrator feels impelled to comment:

> And treweliche, as writen wel I finde
> That al this thing was said of good entente,
> And that hir herte trewe was and kinde
> Towardes him, and spak right as she mente;
> And that she starf for wo neigh whan she wente,
> And was in purpos evere to be trewe:
> Thus writen they that of hir werkes knewe. (1415–21)

This is the first time in the poem that the narrator has taken an opportunity to point to a discrepancy between Criseide's words and her future action—his first overt invocation of dramatic irony. This suggests a slight shift in his attitude toward her. Hitherto he has in his own person tried to keep Criseide as remote as he can from the charges set down in the old books. But now his use of the old books to find evidence that will serve, if not to excuse her, at least to dull the sharp edges of our judgment of her, suggests that he is coming to terms—though most reluctantly—with the inevitability of her infidelity. His love for her is no less, but it needs more support. The present passage is the first of several introduced by the adverb *trewely* in which the old books are called as witnesses to some fact that will soften our judgment on Criseide's failure to be true,[1] with the result that *trewely* seems almost to mean 'despite all evidence to the contrary' or 'despite what you are thinking', like the *surely* that scholars sometimes employ to support statements which they suspect their readers will feel to be most unsure.

The departure of Criseide from Troy at the beginning of Book V is described with several inadvertent ambiguities. Diomede is ready to escort her to the Greek camp,

> For sorwe of which she felte hir herte bleede,
> As she that niste what was best to rede.
> And trewely, as men in bookes rede,
> Men wiste nevere womman han the care,
> Ne was so loth out of a town to fare. (v.17–21)

The abortive simile—'As she (or like a woman) who did not know what was best to do'; the assurance, 'And trewely', which raises the doubt it seeks to allay; and finally, the charming imprecision, 'Men never knew a woman so loath to leave a town', a synecdoche in which, according to the logic of love, the town includes Troilus but nevertheless a statement that fails to mention him—all these momentarily seem to lift a curtain that we were perhaps not aware was covering Criseide's heart, only to drop it again before we can see what is behind it. Then on the journey Diomede makes his sudden declaration of love, at the conclusion of which the narrator tells us that

> Criseide unto that purpos lite answerde,
> As she that was with sorwe oppressed so
> That in effect she nought his tales herde,
> But here and ther, now here a word or two. (v.176–9)

Once again we meet the half-simile that instead of directing the imaginative reaction outward keeps it contracted within the literal statement, arousing the sense of difference, but leaving it unsatisfied. Did Criseide herself not hear what Diomede said, or was she like a woman who was so oppressed with sorrow that she—that is, the woman Criseide is like—would not hear what he said? One does not know whether to read the indicative or the subjunctive.

But the narrator continues unequivocally in the indicative:

[1] The adverb *trewely* is unusually common in the last books of *Troilus*: twenty-five occurrences in Books IV and V to thirteen in Books I–III.

> Hire thoughte hir sorweful herte brast atwo,
> For whan she gan hir fader fer espye,
> Wel neigh down of hir hors she gan to sie. (180–2)

In any case, I hope the statement is unequivocal. Yet, at the risk of imitating Thersites and being very unfair to Criseide, I must confess that I don't altogether follow the logic: I don't believe that her nearly slipping from her horse upon seeing her father is very good proof that it seemed to her that her heart was breaking, though that is what the causal conjunction *for* implies. It looks as if the narrator, searching for objective proof of her heart-break and failing to find it, had slipped in the conjunction in order to suggest a *sequitur* where none was readily apparent. In any case, Criseide remains mindful of her manners:

> But nathelees she thanketh Diomede
> Of al his travaile and his goode cheere,
> And that him liste his frendshipe hire to bede,
> And she accepteth it in good manere,
> And wol do fain that is him lief and dere,
> And trusten him she wolde, and wel she mighte,
> As saide she; and from hir horse sh'alighte. (183–9)

How much of this answer is to the purpose of Diomede's offer of love is a question best left to individual judgment, but it is rather less malapropos than one might have expected from a woman who has just heard a word or two, here and there, of what he said. There are six and a half lines of it—an adequate number—and it at least has the effect of keeping her safely on her horse, for at the end of it she is able to alight with no accompanying cries of 'Look to the lady!' In response to her father's welcome

> She saide eek she was fain with him to meete,
> And stood forth muwet, milde, and mansuete. (193–4)

And there the narrator leaves her, saying nothing but managing to do so mildly and courteously, grief-stricken but wholly self-possessed—a charming enigma.

This is the last time we see Criseide self-possessed, for from now on she is entirely dedicated to grief. When she next appears, it is the ninth day after the lovers' separation—at least, that is what it is in Troy: it is not clear what day it is in the Greek camp, but this hardly matters, since Criseide's soliloquies make it clear enough that she has no resources that will enable her to return to the city. She is indeed a piteous sight, and in one egregiously sentimental stanza the narrator interrupts his description of her to assure us—even without recourse to his old books—that any one on earth would have wept to see her grief. But while the emotional atmosphere is humid with tears, it is apparent that Criseide's sorrow has lost its specific cause and become generalized. Instead of appearing as a woman who is suffering because of separation from her lover, she has become a conventional damsel-in-distress, for whom we are to feel sorry because she is alone, 'With wommen fewe among the Greekes stronge'. It is for this reason indeed that she is feeling sorry for herself. The narrator's tender explanation,

> And this was yit the worste of al hir paine:
> Ther was no wight to whom she dorste hire plaine, (727-8)

while it presumably implies how greatly she misses Troilus, also suggests, unhappily, how useful she might find Diomede.

There follows another futile soliloquy in which Criseide resolves to return to Troy 'bitide what bitide . . . tomorwe at night', and despite what people may think of her. When she repeats the vow,

> For which, withouten any wordes mo,
> To Troye I wol, as for conclusioun, (764-5)

the narrator gives her the lie, the only time in the course of the entire poem that he shows ill temper with her:

> But God it woot, er fully monthes two,
> She was ful fer fro that entencioun:
> For bothe Troilus and Troye town
> Shal knottelees thurghout hir herte slide—
> For she wol take a purpos for t'abide. (766-70)

After this direct rebuke, the narrator turns to Diomede, who, despite his outward self-assurance, can hardly persuade himself that he will be able to win Criseide. Then follow the three portraits—Diomede, Criseide, Troilus—that have been discussed so often that I shall pass over them,[1] pausing only to observe again

---

[1] Criseide's portrait is discussed in a slightly different context above, pp. 57-9.

that the portrait of Criseide, so immensely remote in tone, containing so strange a mixture of the trivial and the essential, concludes with one of Chaucer's most striking anticlimaxes:

> Ne nevere mo ne lakked hire pitee:
> Tendre-herted, sliding of corage. (824–5)

All three of the qualities ascribed to her have to do with the
heart, but the fine potentialities inherent in the first two, pity
and tender-heartedness, are undone by the third, instability of
heart, so briefly and unemphatically stated. The anticlimax of
Criseide's character, which is both the image of and reason for
the anticlimax that the whole poem becomes, is heightened by
the narrator's irrelevant apology:

> But trewely I can nat telle hir age. (826)

In this passage he seems to be trying to pick up the pieces of
Criseide—the one giving her age has eluded him—before putting
them back in their box. One expects that he will hurry over the
details of her infidelity and get back to Troilus. Indeed, it would
have been kinder of him to have done so. Instead, however, he
takes pains to try to salvage something from the ruins of her
character, with the unhappy result that he finally leaves her in
greater ignominy than if he had not made the attempt. I say
'unhappy result' because I am sure the narrator would have
been unhappy if he had realized the effect he was producing;
but I believe that Chaucer himself must have derived much
satisfaction from the dazzling series of anticlimaxes that he
allows his narrator to achieve with Criseide, and if I sound even
more like Thersites than I have done before, I shall blame it on
the poet himself.

The three portraits concluded, the narrator tells us of Diomede's visit to Criseide on the tenth day. She welcomes him,
places him beside her, serves him wine, and they chat about this
and that as friends do when they meet. Then Diomede makes
the long speech in which he woos Criseide with a combination of
threat and boast. The narrator breaks in on it angrily:

> What sholde I telle his wordes that he saide?
> He spak ynough for oo day at the meeste.
> It preveth wel: he spak so that Criseide

> Graunted on the morwe, at his requeste,
> For to speken with him at the leeste—
> So that he nolde speke of swich matere.
> And thus to him she saide as ye mowe heere. (946–52)

But despite the implied colon after the last line, Criseide's answer does not follow at once. Perhaps the narrator is aware that some of the indignation he has just shown for Diomede has spilled over on to Criseide, so that he must take a few lines to counteract the effect:

> As she that hadde hir herte on Troilus
> So faste that ther may it noon arace;
> And straungely she spak, and saide thus. (953–5)

Regardless of what the narrator intended, his imprecision here is fatal. The simile which is not a simile finally realizes the full potential it has, I think, always had of suggesting the opposite of what it purports to be saying—of turning its own sense inside out. Criseide spoke *like* a woman who loved Troilus, but she was most imperfectly like a woman who loved him, as her speech shows. She spoke *straungely*: the expected sense, given in the *OED* for this line, is 'distantly', 'coldly', 'like a stranger'—to Diomede, that is. But the other sense of the word, 'peculiarly', 'queerly', is not out of place, for the speech she makes is very strange, an extraordinary example of emotional casuistry. It seems as if one half of each stanza were devoted to her love of Troy and the other half to her admiration for Greeks, with the Greeks coming out slightly ahead. It suggests not a woman whose heart is so firmly set on Troilus that no one could pull it away, but one who, in the interests of practicality, is finding reasons for making a spontaneous transfer of heart. Indeed, had Thersites been listening, he would have had every right to conclude that her mind had now turned whore.

Thereafter Diomede 'al fresshly newe ayain Gan preessen on', and obtained her glove.

> And finally, whan it was waxen eve,
> And al was wel, he roos and took his leve. (1014–15)

There follows one of the most delightful stanzas in the poem:

> The brighte Venus folwed and ay taughte
> The way there brode Phebus down alighte;
> And Cynthia hir charhors overraughte
> To whirle out of the Leon if she mighte;
> And Signifer his candeles sheweth brighte,
> Whan that Criseide unto hir bedde wente,
> Inwith hir fadres faire brighte tente. (1016–22)

The sun has set and Venus the evening star is following the sun's setting course toward the horizon; the moon is hastening to spin out of the house of the Lion; and the stars are shining bright. All these deities and planets, all this celestial machinery in grandiose motion merely in order to get a sorry little woman, loving but no Venus, bright-haired but no sun, to bed in the security of her father's tent. On the tenth night, when she had promised she would be back in Troy, this tent seems suddenly fair and bright, Greek though it is. All this cosmic fuss coming to so little, as high romantic aspirations come to so little, and as Criseide comes to so little.

But even this is not the end of her. In the next stanza we see her carefully considering the words of Diomede, his high position, Troy's danger, and her own friendlessness:

> . . . and thus bigan to breede
> The cause why—the soothe for to telle—
> That she took fully purpos for to dwelle. (1027–9)

As is usual in this part of the poem, Criseide's specific thoughts and actions seem, emotionally speaking, anticlimactic. We have been asked to bear with her too long, and because we know what she is going to do so well that we feel as if she had done it, we become impatient with her going through the motions of deliberation. And the narrator is aware of what is happening to the reader, for in the next stanza, after telling us that 'gostly for to speke' Diomede came to Criseide the next morning, he acknowledges our impatience and submits to its demands:

> And shortly, lest that ye my tale breke,
> So wel he for himselven spak and saide
> That alle hir sikes sore adown he laide;
> And finally, the soothe for to sayne,
> He refte hire of the grete of al hir paine. (1032–6)

But even in submitting, he increases our sense of anticlimax. Diomede is said to have done two things for Criseide, and the second is expressed as if it were of a different order from the first: he caused all her grievous sighs to abate, and then finally, to tell the truth,[1] he relieved her of the chief part of her pain. Perhaps there is an essential difference between curing some one's sighs and curing some one's pain, though if so it escapes me. In response to his own emotions, the narrator is trying to slow up the process of Criseide's surrender at the very time when, in response to the reader's impatience, he seems to be speeding it up.

And when did the complete surrender occur? On the eleventh morning, if we are to believe what we have just read. But in the next stanzas we are allowed to see into a future of sweet, reluctant, amorous delay indefinitely prolonged:

> And after this the storye telleth us
> That she him yaf the faire baye steede,
> The which he ones wan of Troilus;
> And eek a brooch—and that was litel neede—
> That Troilus was, she yaf this Diomede;
> And eek, the bet from sorwe him to releve,
> She made him were a pencel of hir sleeve.
>
> I finde eek in the stories elleswhere,
> Whan thurgh the body hurt was Diomede
> Of Troilus, tho wepte she many a tere
> Whan that she sawgh his wide woundes bleede;
> And that she took to keepen him good heede,
> And for to helen him of his sorwes smerte. (1037–50)

A steed; Troilus' brooch; a pencel of her sleeve; tears for a wound from Troilus; and loving care to cure it. Yet the list is not complete:

> Men sayn—I noot—that she yaf him hir herte.

Anticlimax upon anticlimax. It is true that the gifts Criseide gave to Diomede are roughly in ascending order of importance,

---

[1] In recounting Criseide's ultimate infidelity the narrator seems to be having the truth squeezed out of him: in addition to 'gostly for to speke' (1030), note 'the soothe for to sayn' (1012), 'the soothe for to telle' (1028), and 'the soothe for to sayne' (1035).

and that none is as important as her heart. But there is a logic in the weight of numbers as well as in order of magnitude, and after a woman has given her lover a number of gifts, it is fairly safe to assume that her heart has gone along with them: otherwise she's either heartless or a whore. But the assumption is not safe for the narrator: 'Men say she gave him her heart, but I don't know'.

Attempting until the very end to present the best side of Criseide, the narrator introduces her final speech with the words,

> But trewely, the storye telleth us
> Ther made nevere womman more wo
> Than she, whan that she falsed Troilus. (1051–2)

And her speech is indeed an anguished one: seldom has self-pity been more pitifully expressed, though all she really says is, 'Why did all this have to happen to me?' Having surrendered to circumstances, she salvages what she can of her lost integrity with the resolution, 'To Diomede, algate, I wol be trewe', and then, to a touching farewell to her absent former lover she adds the consoling words, 'But al shal passe, and thus I take my leve'. Earlier the narrator had narrowly missed making an inadvertent identification of Criseide with Fortune; here she finally makes it herself.

Yet the narrator makes one last attempt to mitigate her perfidy:

> But trewely, how longe it was bitweene
> That she forsook him for this Diomede,
> Ther is noon auctour telleth it, I weene.
> Take every man now to his bookes heede:
> He shal no terme finden, out of drede;
> For though that he bigan to wowe hire soone,
> Er he hire wan yit was ther more to doone. (1086–92)

'But trewely', despite what you may be thinking, none of the old books says how long it took Criseide to forsake Troilus for Diomede—and we are invited to go to our libraries in order to document the fact that no specific period is mentioned, not even the 'er fully monthes two' that the narrator himself has earlier stated, during his one moment of pique with his heroine. Having squeezed what he now suggests was a long time into three stanzas, he seems to expect us to recall our emotional responses and reassort them so as to suit an extended timetable. We are unlikely to do so, just as we are unlikely to be impressed by his final couplet:

> For though that he bigan to wowe hire soone,
> Er he hire wan yit was ther more to doone.

This is the narrator's last rhetorical failure. As he had done earlier when Criseide was falling in love with Troilus, he has chosen to express himself in the form of a common saying, in which understatement is supposedly compensated for by sententiousness of tone. Under the circumstances, however, no magnification of the literal sense is effected; the statement remains uninformative: there was more to do, but how much? And, indeed, why do we care, since it has all been done long ago as far as our emotions are concerned?

There follows the narrator's rather unnecessary remark that he does not wish to chide this 'sely' woman further than the story requires. Her infamy is so widely known that it should suffice for punishment.

> And if I mighte excuse hire any wise,
> For she so sory was for hir untrouthe,
> Ywis, I wolde excuse hire yit for routhe. (1097–99)

There is nothing left to do but to pity her, remembering her own quality of pity. The last action that Criseide takes in the poem is ascribed to pity. Troilus writes to her, begging her to keep her promise to return to Troy.

> For which Criseide upon a day for routhe—
> I take it so—touching al this matere
> Wroot him ayain— (1587–9)

wrote him one of the most poisonously hypocritical letters in the annals of literature, one in which, with exquisitely selfish cruelty, she refuses to admit to him that she no longer loves him or intends ever to come back. This the narrator takes for pity.

It seems acceptable to say that Criseide is a very complex woman—at least I hope it is, for I've said it often enough. Yet it might be better to say that Criseide's character, if any, is a complex composite of emotional responses to her that the poem has evoked from the reader and continues to evoke after he has finished reading. You will recall what Pandarus replies when he is finally forced by Troilus to admit that his niece has proved unfaithful:

> What sholde I sayn? I hate, ywis, Criseide,
> And God woot I wol hate hire everemore. (1732–3)

But Troilus himself, just a moment before, has addressed himself to his absent mistress thus:

> Thurgh which I see that clene out of youre minde
> Ye han me caste—and I ne can nor may,
> For al this world, withinne myn herte finde
> To unloven you a quarter of a day.
> In cursed time I born was, wailaway,
> That you, that doon me al this wo endure,
> Yit love I best of any creature. (1695–8)

These are the two simple attitudes to Criseide that Chaucer has carefully nurtured—simple, but in combination infinitely complex. One of the principal ways he has nurtured them is through his narrator, making him so wholly loving of Criseide that he will do anything to excuse her, and then seeing to it that in the very process of excusing her he will suggest—sometimes most unfairly—reasons for us to distrust and hate her. Yet, of course, the logic of fact—the logic of Pandarus—never succeeds in undoing the logic of love—the logic of Troilus and the narrator. It is sensible to hate what you have loved when it betrays you; but it is human to go on loving it if it once seemed better than anything you had known before, giving you glimpses of a world where experience is most rich and intense. Criseide is so memorable a character because she evokes from us simultaneously the most powerful emotions of which we are capable, if the most opposed. Psychologically, we are never allowed to form any very precise or consistent image of her; indeed we are actively prevented from doing so. Yet because we know people not really with our minds but with our hearts, every sensitive reader will feel that he really knows Criseide—and no sensible reader will ever claim that he really understands her.

6

THE ENDING OF
'TROILUS'

ONE OF CHAUCER's familiar pretences is that he is a versifier utterly devoted to simplicity of meaning—for the reason that he considers himself, apparently, utterly incapable of complexity. He defines his poetic mission as the reporting of facts in tolerable verse, and he implies that that's hard enough to do. True poetry may, for all of him, do something much better but it is not clear to Chaucer exactly what it is or how it does it. He and *ars poetica* are, to be sure, on parallel roads, moving in the same direction; but the roads are a long way apart and are destined to meet, perhaps, not even in infinity. On the one hand, Chaucer, reciting his simple stories 'in swich Englissh as he can'; on the other, poetry, penetrating regions of complex significance far beyond the grasp of a simple straightforward versifier.

Chaucer's pretended inferiority complex on the subject of poetry must have stemmed from something real in his own life probably connected with his being a bourgeois writing for high-born members of the royal court. What interests me now however, is not the origin of the pose, but its literary value. For I think that Chaucer discovered in the medieval modesty convention a way of poetic life: that, by constantly assuring us, both through direct statement and through implication, of his inability to write anything but the simplest kind of verse, Chaucer creates just that poetry of complex significance that he disclaims striving for. In this paper I shall focus attention on the last stanzas of *Troilus*, where it seems to me that a kind of dramatization of his poetic ineptitude achieves for him a poetic success that not many poets in any language have attained. But I shall first consider briefly some characteristic Chaucerian 'ineptitudes' in his other works.

Modesty is endemic both with Chaucer in his own first person—whoever that is—and with his dramatic creations: none of them can do much in the way of poetry. Like the Squire, they cannot climb over so high a stile, or, like his father, they set out to plough, God wot, a large field with weak oxen; or, if they are not ploughing a field, they're gleaning it, like the author of the Prologue to the *Legend of Good Women*, and are full glad of any kernel that their talented predecessors have missed. Or else, like the Prioress, they are so afflicted by infantilism that they speak no better than a child of twelvemonth old, or less. Like the Merchant and the Franklin, they are rude men, 'burel' men, they cannot glose, they have no rhetoric, they call a spade a spade; they come after even such second-rate poets as that fellow Chaucer, bearing only *hawe bake*—pig food—and are reduced to prose, like the Man of Law in his Prologue. They can't even get the data down in the right order, like the Monk or like the narrator of the Prologue to the *Canterbury Tales*. Or, worst of all, as in the case of the pilgrim who recites the romance of Sir Thopas, their inability to frame a story of their own makes them resort to 'a rim I lerned longe agoon', and when that is shot down in mid-flight, they have to take refuge in one of the most anaesthetic sermons that ever mortified a reader. If it is dramatically appropriate that they be capable rhetoricians, like the Clerk, they comply at once with a decree that declares high style to be inappropriate to their audience. In short, they seldom admit to more than a nodding acquaintance with the Muse.

The normal function of the modesty convention is, I suppose, to prepare a pleasant surprise for the reader when the poem turns out better than he has been led to expect, or, at worst, to save him disappointment when the implied warning is fulfilled. This latter alternative is perhaps valid in some of Chaucer's tales, notably the Monk's. But the really important function of the modesty convention in Chaucer is to prepare a soil in which complexity of meaning may grow most fruitfully. That is, the narrator's assertion, implicit or explicit, of his devotion to the principle of simplicity, his denial of regard for possible

7—S.O.C.

complexity, results, by a curious paradox, *in* complexity; for the harder he tries to simplify issues, the less amenable to simplification they become, and, in artistic terms, the more complex and suggestive the poem becomes. To epitomize, the typical Chaucerian narrator begins by assuring you, either by a modesty prologue or by the notable simplicity of his manner—sometimes by both—that in what you are about to hear there will be nothing but the most straightforward presentation of reality: the narrator's feet are firmly on the ground, but he is no poet, and his control of anything but fact is weak. Subsequently the poet Chaucer, working from behind the narrator, causes to arise from this hard ground a complex of possible meanings, endlessly dynamic and interactive, amplifying, qualifying, even denying the simple statement: these draw much of their vitality from the fact that they exist—or seem to exist—either unknown to or in spite of the narrator; indeed, the latter sometimes betrays an uneasy awareness that the poem has got out of hand and is saying something he doesn't approve of or at least didn't intend, and his resistance to this meaning may well become an important part of it. That is, the ultimate significance of the poem derives much from the tension between the narrator's simple statement and the complex of implications that have arisen to qualify it.

The Chaucer who tells of the pilgrimage to Canterbury provides an obvious example of this tension between the simple and the complex. At the very beginning of the Prologue he lets us know exactly what we may expect of his narrative—namely what he saw with his own two eyes, and not an adverb more. And, as I have tried to show elsewhere,[1] his prospectus itself is a miracle of stylistic simplicity, its pedestrian matter-of-factness supporting by example the limited poetic ideal that it is expressing. Yet it is because he has succeeded in persuading the reader to expect no more than meets the eye that, when he comes to the portrait of the Prioress,[2] the poet is able to reveal to us the profoundest depths of that rather shallow lady. The narrator, to be sure, describes her flatly as he saw her, and what he saw was attractive, and it attracted the warm fervour of his

[1] See above, pp. 46–7.
[2] For further discussion of this portrait, see above, pp. 3–4 and 59–64.

love; but what he did not see was that everything he did see amounted to a well-indexed catalogue of the Prioress's short-comings, which seen coldly would produce a kind of travesty of a Prioress. But because of his love for the woman, he is un-aware of the satirical potential of his portrait, so that this po-tential, while always imminent, is never actually realized. One feels that if any one had pointed it out to the narrator, he would have been horrified, as, indeed, the Prioress would have been horrified if any one had pointed it out to her—and as even today certain readers are horrified when one points it out to them. And quite rightly, too, because of the great love that permeates the simple description. But the effect achieved by means of a narrator who resists complexity is of a highly complex strife between love and satire, between wholehearted approval and heartless criticism. These are factors which in logic would cancel one another, as a negative cancels a positive; but in poetry they exist forever side by side—as they also do in reality wherever there are ladies at once so attractive and so fallible as the Pri-oress. Indeed, the two factors, love and satire, unite with one another to form a third meaning—one which both qualifies and enhances the Prioress's own motto, *amor vincit omnia*, by suggesting something of the complex way in which love does conquer all. This occurs because the narrator, incapable of complexity, adheres rigorously to the presentation of simple fact.

The ways in which Chaucerian narrators enhance the mean-ing of their stories by missing the point of them are various. Occasionally, indeed, a narrator will rise up in the pulpit sen-tentiously to point *out* or at least to point *to* what he takes to be his real meaning. The only trouble is that his aim is likely to be poor: he will suggest a meaning which, while it bears some logical relation to the ultimate significance, is at best no more than gross over-simplification. For instance, the Nun's Priest, at the end of his remarkably verbose epic of Chauntecleer, solemnly addresses his audience:

> Lo, swich it is for to be recchelees
> And necligent, and truste on flaterye.
> But ye that holden this tale a folye,
> As of a fox, or of a cok and hen,
> Taketh the moralitee, goode men. (B²3736–40)

He then goes on to quote St Paul in a way that suggests that
doctrine is produced every time a pen inscribes words on paper—
a thought most comforting to an author hard put to determine
his own meaning. With Pauline authority on his side, the Nun's
Priest exhorts us:

> Taketh the fruit, and lat the chaf be stille. (B²3443)

Now all this certainly bids us find a simple moral in the story;
but, so far as I know, no two critics have ever found the same
moral: most agree only in rejecting the Nun's Priest's stated
moral about negligence and flattery. The reason for this disagreement is, as I have tried to suggest elsewhere,[1] that the real
moral of the Tale is in the chaff—the rhetorical amplifications
which make of Chauntecleer a good representative of western
man trying to maintain his precarious dignity in the face of a
universe and of a basic avian (or human) nature which fail to
co-operate with him. But the Nun's Priest, characteristically,
suggests this moral only by pointing towards another which
satisfies nobody.

Another Canterbury narrator, the Knight, similarly asks us
to take a simple view of a story which is really very complex.
After describing the languishing of Arcite in Theban exile and
of Palamon in Athenian prison, both of them quite out of the
running in their race for Emily, the narrator finishes off the first
part of his poem with a *demande d'amour*:

> You loveres axe I now this questioun:
> Who hath the worse, Arcite or Palamoun? (A1347–8)

With this tidy rhetorical flourish the Knight suggests that his
story is a simple one about a rivalry in love. The question
invites the reader to take sides in this rivalry, to feel sorrier for
one youth than the other, and hence to choose a favourite for
the contest that is to come. He appeals, that is, to our sense of
justice. Until recently, the majority of Chaucerian critics put
their money on Palamon; and since at the end of the story
Providence accords him Emily and lets him live happily ever
after, while it buries Arcite, this majority have naturally felt

---

[1] See *Chaucer's Poetry*, pp. 940–4; also 'Patristic Exegesis in the Criticism of
Medieval Literature: The Opposition', below, pp. 146–50.

that justice has operated in an exemplary manner, and nothing is pleasanter than to see justice behave itself. Yet there has always been a noisy group—with whom I deeply sympathize—who feel that Arcite is very badly treated by the story. This disagreement represents a kind of protracted response to the Knight's rhetorical question.

The lack of critical agreement, however, once again suggests that there is something wrong both about the question and about the debate. If intelligent readers cannot agree on which of the two young men is the more deserving, then there is probably not much difference between them. And indeed, the way the poem carefully balances their claims bears this out. On temperamental grounds you may prefer a man who mistakes his lady for Venus to a man who knows a woman when he sees one, or you may not; but such preference has no moral validity. The poem concerns something larger than the young men's relative deserts, though it is something closely related to that question. Recognition of their equality leads to the conclusion that the poem does not assert the simple triumph of justice when Palamon ends up with Emily, nor the triumph of a malignant anti-justice when Arcite ends up in his cold grave, alone. What it does suggest—and I think with every syllable of its being—is that Providence is not working justly, so far as we can see, when it kills Arcite, nor, so far as we can see, unjustly when it lets Palamon live happily ever after. For no matter how hard we look, we cannot hope to see why Providence behaves as it does; all we can do is our best, making a virtue of necessity, enjoying what is good, and remaining cheerful.

But to most of us this is an unpalatable moral, far less appealing than the one which will result if only we can promote Palamon into an unchallenged position of deserving; and it is a very stale bit of cold cabbage indeed unless it is as hard-won as the Knight's own battles. The experience by which the individual attains the Knight's tempered view of life is an important part of that view, and renders it, if not palatable, digestible and nourishing. This experience must include our questioning of relative values, our desire to discover that even-handed justice does prevail in the universe, and our resistance to the conclusion that justice, so far as we can see, operates at best with only one hand. The emotional history of the ultimate conclusion makes it valid; and the way the Knight's question is framed, pointing at what we should like to believe, and through that at what we shall have to believe, causes us to share in that experience—leads us through the simple to the complex.

It is at the end of *Troilus* that Chaucer, employing the kind of devices I have been discussing, achieves his most complex poetic effect. His narrator has worked hard, from the very beginning, to persuade us of his simplicity, though from the very beginning his simplicity has been compromised by the fact that, apparently unknown to himself, he wavers between two quite different—though equally simple—attitudes towards his story. It is the saddest story in the world, and it is the gladdest story in the world. This double attitude appears strongly in the opening stanzas, when he tells us that his motive for writing is, paradoxically, to bring honour to Love and gladden lovers with a love story so sad that his verses shed tears while he writes them and that Tisiphone is his only appropriate Muse. Yet though he starts out firmly resolved to relate the double sorrow of Troilus

> . . . in loving of Criseide,
> And how that she forsook him er she deide, (*TC* 1.55–6)

as the story progresses he seems to forget all about the second sorrow. The historical perspective, which sees before and after and knows the sad ending, gives way to the limited, immediate view of one who loves the actors in the story, and in his love pines for what is not so desperately that he almost brings it into being. The scholar's motive for telling a sad story simply because it is true finds itself at war with the sentimentalist's motive of telling a love story simply because it is happy and beautiful. The optimism that one acquires when one lives with people so attractive makes a gay future for all seem inevitable. Once launched upon the love story, the narrator refuses to look forward to a future that the scholar in him knows to be already sadly past; at moments when the memory of that sad future breaks in on him, he is likely to deny his own sources, and to suggest that, despite the historical evidence to the contrary,

Criseide was, perhaps, not unfaithful at all—men have been lying about her.[1]

For the greater part of the poem the intimately concerned, optimistic narrator is in full control of the story—or rather, the story is in full control of him, and persuades him that a world that has such people in it is not only the best of all possible worlds, but the most possible. When in the fifth book the facts of history force him back towards the historical perspective, which has always known that his happiness and that of the lovers were transitory, illusory, he does his best to resist the implications arising from his ruined story—tries to circumvent them, denies them, slides off them. Thus an extraordinary feeling of tension, even of dislocation, develops from the strife in the narrator's mind between what should be and what was—and hence what is. This tension is the emotional storm-centre which causes the narrator's various shifts and turns in his handling of the ending, and which also determines the great complexity of the poem's ultimate meaning.

So skilfully has Chaucer mirrored his narrator's internal warfare—a kind of nervous breakdown in poetry—that many a critic has concluded that Chaucer himself was bewildered by his poem. One, indeed, roundly condemns the whole fifth book, saying that it reads like 'an earlier draft . . . which its author lacked sufficient interest to revise'. According to this critic, Chaucer 'cannot bring himself to any real enthusiasm for a plot from which the bright lady of his own creation has vanished'. And, elsewhere, 'What had happened to the unhappy Criseyde and to her equally unhappy creator was that the story in which they were involved had betrayed them both'.[2] Now this is, in a rather sad way, the ultimate triumph of Chaucer's method. The critic responds with perfect sympathy to the narrator's bewilderment, even to the extent of seeming to suggest that the poet had written four-fifths of his story before he discovered how it came out. But in fact Chaucer's warmly sympathetic narrator has blinded the critic's eyes as effectively as he had blinded his own. It is not true that the bright lady of Chaucer's

---

[1] *TC* IV.20-I.
[2] Marchette Chute, *Geoffrey Chaucer of England* (London, 1946), pp. 179, 180, and 178.

creation has vanished—Criseide is still very much present in book five. What has vanished is the bright dream of the enduring power of human love, and in a burst of creative power that it is not easy to match elsewhere.

For the *moralitee* of *Troilus and Criseide* (and by morality I do not mean 'ultimate meaning') is simply this: that human love, and by a sorry corollary everything human, is unstable and illusory. I give the moral so flatly now because in the remainder of this paper I shall be following the narrator in his endeavour to avoid it, and indeed shall be eagerly abetting him in trying to avoid it, and even pushing him away when he finally accepts it. I hope in this way to suggest how Chaucer, by manipulating his narrator, achieves an objective image of the poem's significance that at once greatly qualifies and enhances this moral, and one that is, of course, far more profound and less absolute than my flat-footed statement. The meaning of the poem is not the moral, but a complex qualification of the moral.

Let us turn now to that part of the poem, containing the last eighteen stanzas, which is often referred to by modern scholars, though not by the manuscripts, as the Epilogue. I object to the term because it implies that this passage was tacked on to the poem after the poet had really finished his work, so that it is critically if not physically detachable from what has gone before.[1] And while I must admit that the nature of this passage, its curious twists and turns, its occasional air of fecklessness, set it off from what has gone before, it also seems to me to be the head of the whole body of the poem.[2]

The last intimately observed scene of the action is the final, anticlimactic interview between Troilus and Pandarus, wherein the latter is driven by the sad logic of his loyalty and of his pragmatism to express hatred of his niece, and to wish her dead. Pandarus's last words are, 'I can namore saye', and it is now up to the narrator, who is as heart-broken as Troilus and Pan-

---

[1] The extreme exponent of detachability is W. C. Curry in his well-known essay, 'Destiny in *Troilus and Criseyde*', *PMLA*, xlv (1930), 129 ff., reprinted in his *Chaucer and the Mediaeval Sciences* (second revised and enlarged ed., 1960): see especially pp. 294–8.

[2] I believe that this is the opinion of many Chaucerians. See, e.g., Dorothy Everett, *Essays on Middle English Literature* (1955), pp. 134–8, and Dorothy Bethurum, 'Chaucer's Point of View as Narrator', *PMLA*, lxxiv (1959), 516–18.

darus, to express the significance of his story. His first reaction is to take the epic high road; by means of the exalted style to reinvest Troilus with the human dignity that his unhappy love has taken from him. The narrator starts off boldly enough:

> Greet was the sorwe and plainte of Troilus;
> But forth hire cours Fortune ay gan to holde.
> Criseide loveth the sone of Tydeüs,
> And Troilus moot weepe in cares colde. (*TC* v.1744-7)

But though the manner is epic, the subject is not: an Aeneas in Dido's pathetic plight is no fit subject for Virgilian style. And the narrator, overcome by the pathos of his story, takes refuge in moralization:

> Swich is this world, whoso it can biholde:
> In eech estaat is litel hertes reste—
> God leve us for to take it for the beste!

How true! And how supremely, brilliantly, inadequate! It has been said that all experience does no more than prove some platitude or other, but one hopes that poetic experience will do more, or in any case that poetry will not go from pathos to bathos. This moral, the trite moral of the Monk's Tale—Isn't life awful?—which the Monk arrives at—again and again— *a priori* would be accepted by many a medieval man as a worthy moral for the *Troilus,* and the narrator is a medieval man. But the poet behind the narrator is aware that an experience that has been intimately shared—not merely viewed historically, as are the Monk's tragedies—requires not a moral, but a meaning arrived at *a posteriori*, something earned, and in a sense new. Moreover, the narrator seems still to be asking the question, Can nothing be salvaged from the wreck of the story? For he goes on once more to have recourse to epic enhancement of his hero, more successfully this time, since it is the martial heroism of Troilus, rather than his unhappy love, that is the subject: there follow two militant stanzas recounting his prowess and his encounters with Diomede. But again the epic impulse fails, for the narrator's real subject is not war but unhappy love, for which epic values will still do nothing—will neither salvage the dignity of Troilus nor endow his experience with meaning. In a wistful stanza, the narrator faces his failure to do by epic style what he desires to have done:

> And if I hadde ytaken for to write
> The armes of this ilke worthy man,
> [But, unfortunately, *arma virumque non cano*]
> Than wolde ich of his batailes endite;
> But for that I to writen first bigan
> Of his love, I have said as I can—
> His worthy deedes, whoso list hem heere,
> Rede Dares—he can telle hem alle yfere. (1765–71)

This sudden turn from objective description to introspection mirrors the narrator's quandary. Unable to get out of his hopeless predicament, he does what we all tend to do when we are similarly placed: he begins to wonder why he ever got himself into it. The sequel of this unprofitable speculation is likely to be panic, and the narrator very nearly panics when he sees staring him in the face another possible moral for the love poem he has somehow been unwise enough to recite. The moral that is staring him in the face is written in the faces of the ladies of his audience, the anti-feminist moral which is at once obvious and, from a court poet, unacceptable:

> Biseeching every lady bright of hewe,
> And every gentil womman what she be,
> That al be that Criseide was untrewe,
> That for that gilt she nat be wroth with me.
> Ye may hir giltes in othere bookes see;
> And gladlier I wol write, if you leste,
> Penelopeës trouthe and good Alceste.

While anticipating the ladies' objections, the narrator has, with that relief only a true coward can appreciate, glimpsed a possible way out: denial of responsibility for what the poem says. He didn't write it in the first place, it has nothing to do with him, and anyhow he would much rather have written about faithful women. These excuses are, of course, very much in the comic mood of the Prologue to the *Legend of Good Women* where Alceste, about whom he would prefer to have written, defends him from Love's wrath on the grounds that, being no more than a translator, he wrote about Criseide 'from inno-

cence, and knew not what he said'. And if he can acquit himself
of responsibility for Criseide by pleading permanent inanity,
there is no reason why he cannot get rid of all his present ten-
sions by funnelling them into a joke against himself. This he
tries to do by turning upside down the anti-feminist moral of
the story:

> N'I saye nat this al only for thise men,
> But most for wommen that bitraised be ...

And I haven't recited this exclusively for men, but also, or rather
but mostly, for women who are betrayed

> Thrugh false folk—God yive hem sorwe, amen!—
> That with hir grete wit and subtiltee
> Bitraise you; and this commeveth me
> To speke, and in effect you alle I praye,
> Beeth war of men, and herkneth what I saye.

The last excursion into farce—in a poem that contains a good
deal of farce—is this outrageous inversion of morals, which
even so has a grotesque relevance if all human love, both male
and female, is in the end to be adjudged unstable. With the
narrator's recourse to comedy the poem threatens to end. At
any rate, he asks it to go away:

> Go, litel book, go, litel myn tragedye,
> Ther God thy makere yit, er that he die,
> So sende might to make in som comedye....

(Presumably a comedy will not blow up in his face as this story
has, and will let him end on a note like the one he has just
sounded.) There follows the celebrated injunction of the poet
to his book not to vie with other poetry, but humbly to kiss the
steps of Virgil, Ovid, Homer, Lucan, and Statius. This is the
modesty convention again, but transmuted, I believe, into
something close to arrogance. Perhaps the poem is not to be
classed with the works of these great poets, but I do not feel
that the narrator succeeds in belittling his work by mentioning
it in connection with them; there is such a thing as inviting
comparison by eschewing comparison. It seems that the narrator has abandoned his joke, and is taking his 'little book'—of

more than 8,000 lines—seriously. Increasing gravity characterizes the next stanza, which begins with the hope that the
text will not be miswritten nor mismetred by scribes and lesser
breeds without the law of final -*e*. Then come two lines of
emphatic prayer:

> And red wherso thou be, or elles songe,
> That thou be understonde, God I biseeche.

It is perhaps inconsiderate of the narrator to implore us to
take his sense when he has been so irresolute about defining
his sense. But the movement of the verse now becomes sure and
strong, instead of uncertain and aimless, as the narrator moves
confidently towards a meaning.

For in the next stanza, Troilus meets his death. This begins—
once again—in the epic style, with perhaps a glance at the *Iliad*:

> The wratthe, as I bigan you for to saye,
> Of Troilus the Greekes boughten dere.

Such dignity as the high style can give is thus, for the last time,
proffered Troilus. But for him there is to be no last great battle
in the West, and both the stanza, and Troilus's life, end in
pathos:

> But wailaway, save only Goddes wille:
> Despitously him slow the fierse Achille.

Troilus's spirit at once ascends into the upper spheres whence he
looks down upon this little earth and holds all vanity as compared with the full felicity of heaven. The three stanzas describing Troilus's afterlife afford him that reward which medieval
Christianity allowed to the righteous heathen. And in so doing,
they salvage from the human wreck of the story the human
qualities of Troilus that are of enduring value—most notably,
his *trouthe*, the integrity for which he is distinguished. Moreover,
this recognition by the plot that some human values transcend
human life seems to enable the narrator to come to a definition
of the poem's meaning which he has hitherto been unwilling
to make. Still close to his characters, he witnesses Troilus's rejection of earthly values, and then, apparently satisfied, now that
the mortal good in Troilus has been given immortal reward, he
is willing to make that rejection of *all* mortal goods towards

which the poem has, despite his resistance, been driving him. His rejection occurs—most unexpectedly—in the third of these stanzas. Troilus, gazing down at the earth and laughing within himself at those who mourn his death,

> . . . dampned al oure werk that folweth so
> The blinde lust, the which that may nat laste,
> And sholden al oure herte on hevene caste.

Up until the last line Troilus has been the subject of every main verb in the entire passage; but after he has damned all *our* work, by one of those syntactical ellipses that make Middle English so fluid a language, Troilus's thought is extended to include both narrator and reader: in the last line, *And sholden al oure herte on hevene caste*, the plural verb *sholden* requires the subject *we*; but this subject is omitted, because to the narrator the sequence of the sense is, at last, overpoweringly clear. When, after all his attempts not to have to reject the values inherent in his love story, he finally does reject them, he does so with breath-taking ease.

He does so, indeed, with dangerous ease. Having taken up arms against the world and the flesh, he lays on with a will:

> Swich fin hath, lo, this Troilus for love;
> Swich fin hath al his grete worthinesse;
> Swich fin hath his estaat real above;
> Swich fin his lust, swich fin hath his noblesse;
> Swich fin hath false worldes brotelnesse:
> And thus bigan his loving of Criseide,
> As I have told, and in this wise he deide.

But impressive as this stanza is, its movement is curious. The first five lines express, with increasing force, disgust for a world in which everything—not only what merely *seems* good, but also what really *is* good—comes to nothing in the end. Yet the last two lines,

> And thus bigan his loving of Criseide,
> As I have told, and in this wise he deide,

have, I think, a sweetness of tone that contrasts strangely with the emphatic disgust that precedes them. They seem to express a deep sadness for a doomed potential—as if the narrator,

while forced by the evidence to condemn everything his poem
has stood for, cannot really quite believe that it has come to
nothing. The whole lovely aspiration of the previous action is
momentarily recreated in the spare summary of this couplet.

The sweetness of tone carries over into the next two stanzas,
the much-quoted ones beginning

> O yonge, freshe folkes, he or she,
> In which that love up groweth with youre age,
> Repaireth hoom fro worldly vanitee,
> And of youre herte up casteth the visage
> To thilke God that after his image
> You made; and thinketh al nis but a faire
> This world that passeth soone as flowres faire.

The sweetness here adheres not only to what is being rejected,
but also to what is being sought in its stead, and this marks a
development in the narrator. For he does not now seem so much
to be fleeing away, in despair and disgust, from an ugly world—
the world of the Monk's Tale—as he seems to be moving voluntarily through this world *towards* something infinitely better.
And while this world is a wretched one—ultimately—in which
all love is *feined*, 'pretended' and 'shirked', it is also a world
full of the young potential of human love—'In which that love
up groweth with *oure* age'; a world which, while it passes soon,
passes soon as flowers fair. All the illusory loveliness of a world
which is man's only reality is expressed in the very lines that
reject that loveliness.

In these stanzas the narrator has been brought to the most
mature and complex expression of what is involved in the Christian rejection of the world that seems to be, and indeed is,
man's home, even though he knows there is a better one. But
the narrator himself remains dedicated to simplicity, and makes
one last effort to resolve the tension in his mind between loving
a world he ought to hate and hating a world he cannot help
loving; he endeavours to root out the love:

> Lo, here of payens cursed olde rites;
> Lo, here what alle hir goddes may availe;
> Lo, here thise wrecched worldes appetites;
> Lo, here the fin and guerdon for travaile

> Of Jove, Appollo, of Mars, of swich rascaile;
> Lo, here the forme of olde clerkes speeche
> In poetrye, if ye hir bookes seeche.

For the second time within a few stanzas a couplet has undone
the work of the five lines preceding it. In them is harsh, excessively harsh, condemnation of the world of the poem, including
gods and rites that have played no great part in it. In brilliant
contrast to the tone of these lines is the exhausted calm of the
last two:

> Lo, here the forme of olde clerkes speeche
> In poetrye, if ye hir bookes seeche.

There is a large imprecision about the point of reference of this
couplet. I do not know whether its *Lo here* refers to the five
preceding lines or to the poem as a whole, but I suppose it
refers to the poem as a whole, as the other four *Lo here's* do. If
this is so, then the form of *olde clerkes speeche* is being damned as
well as the *payens cursed olde rites*—by parataxis, at least. Yet
it is not, for the couplet lacks the heavy, fussy indignation of the
earlier lines: instead of indignation there is, indeed, dignity. I
suggest that the couplet once more reasserts, in its simplicity,
all the implicit and explicit human values that the poem has
dealt with, even though these are, to a medieval Christian,
ultimately insignificant. The form of old clerks' speech in poetry
is the sad story that human history tells. It is sad, it is true, it is
lovely, and it is significant, for it is poetry.

This is the last but one of the narrator's searches for a resolution for his poem. I have tried to show how at the end of
Troilus Chaucer has manipulated a narrator capable of only
a simple view of reality in such a way as to achieve the poetic
expression of an extraordinarily complex one. The narrator,
moved by his simple devotion to Troilus, to Pandarus, above
all to Criseide, has been vastly reluctant to find that their story,
so full of the illusion of happiness, comes to nothing—that the
potential of humanity comes to nothing. To avoid this—seemingly simple—conclusion he has done everything he could. He
has tried the epic high road; he has tried the broad highway of
trite moralization; he has tried to eschew responsibility; he

has tried to turn it all into a joke; and all these devices have failed. Finally, with every other means of egress closed, he has subscribed to Troilus's rejection of his own story, though only when, like Gregory when he wept for Trajan, he has seen his desire for his hero's salvation confirmed. Once having made the rejection, he has thrown himself into world-hating with enthusiasm. But now the counterbalance asserts its power. For the same strong love of the world of his story that prevented him from reaching the Christian rejection permeates and qualifies his expression of the rejection. Having painfully climbed close to the top of the ridge he did not want to climb, he cannot help looking back with longing at the darkening but still fair valley in which he lived; and every resolute thrust forward ends with a glance backward. In having his narrator behave thus, Chaucer has achieved a meaning only great poetry can achieve. The world he knows and the heaven he believes in grow ever farther and farther apart as the woeful contrast between them is developed, and ever closer and closer together as the narrator blindly unites them in the common bond of his love. Every false start he has made has amounted, not to a negative, but to a positive; has been a necessary part of the experience without which the moral of the poem would be as meaningless and unprofitable as in the form I gave it a little while ago. The poem states, what much of Chaucer's poetry states, the necessity under which men lie of living in, making the best of, enjoying, and loving a world from which they must remain detached and which they must ultimately hate: a little spot of earth that with the sea embracéd is, as in Book Three Criseide was embraced by Troilus.

For this paradox there is no logical resolution. In the last two stanzas of the poem Chaucer, after asking Gower and Strode for correction, invokes the power that, being supra-logical itself, can alone resolve paradox. He echoes Dante's mighty prayer to the Trinity, 'that al maist circumscrive', and concludes with the lines:

> So make us, Jesus, for thy mercy digne,
> For love of Maide and Moder thyn benigne.

The poem has concerned a mortal woman whose power to love

failed, and it ends with the one mortal woman whose power to love is everlasting. I think it is significant that the prayer of the poem's ending leads up, not to Christ, son of God, but to his mother, daughter of Eve—towards heaven, indeed, but towards heaven through human experience.

7

THE PSYCHOLOGY OF EDITORS OF MIDDLE ENGLISH TEXTS

INSTEAD OF the paper I am about to give[1], Professor Lawlor originally requested a report on the progress of an edition of the B-Text of *Piers Plowman* that Professor George Kane of London and I have been engaged on for some years. Professor Kane and I gave Professor Lawlor an immediate, firm, and unanimous reply: no progress report. Not that we haven't made progress: as a matter of fact, we have made extraordinary progress—that is, from the point where we began; but how close we have come to the end depends upon what one considers the ending point to be. Obviously, publication is the ultimate of ultimates; but the moment when one is ready to go into print is defined less by the existence of a neat, well-checked MS than by the editor's conviction that he has really accomplished something like what he started out to do. But since that was many years ago, when he was younger, when time and energy were seemingly unlimited, and when the word 'definitive' seemed still to have a kinship with the word 'finite', conviction of completion is not easy to attain. Indeed, I suppose it is made possible only by an act of the will—a conscious acceptance of the fact that while the MS is not what one once hoped it was going to be, it probably represents the best that one is going to be able to do in a world where time moves always faster. Completion,

---

[1] This paper was delivered at the IAUPE meeting in Venice in 1965, with Professor John Lawlor in charge of the medieval section.

then, is not so much an objective fact of scholarship as a state of
the editor's psyche; and it seems true that almost all stages of the
editorial process represent psychological achievements as much
as they do scholarly ones: for the fact is that this branch of
scholarly activity, which is often made to appear most austerely
detached and objective, is almost wholly subjective. Thus today
in talking about the psychology of editors of Middle English texts
I hope to make partial reparation to Professor Lawlor for failing
to give a progress report on *Piers Plowman*—though any one who
can determine from my remarks where we are in our edition
is a far better scholar—and psychologist—than I.

I have mentioned the melancholy subject of time, which
is perhaps the chief factor in determining the state of the editorial psyche—or rather, since there is never enough of it, the
chief factor in assuring that the editorial psyche will remain
perpetually in flux. A given line of Middle English poetry has,
let us say, two main variant forms in the MSS; after careful
analysis of the textual situation and long thought about the
meaning, the editor, not unlike a bachelor choosing a bride,
selects Line Form A for his text. For a time he lives in virtuous
serenity, pleased with his decision. A year or more passes, and
then one day it comes to him, like a bolt from the blue, that he
should, of course, have chosen Line Form B; in short, he married
the wrong girl. She is attractive, she is plausible, she has her
points, but he just can't live with her; he lies awake at nights
enumerating her faults, which seem considerable when she is
compared with her rejected rival, who now appears infinitely
preferable. So the editor (who is the least reliable of all possible
husbands) obtains a divorce—an enormously expensive one,
since it forces him to change his apparatus and also to worry
endlessly whether other decisions he has made have not depended on this one (and, as in matrimony, he will find that they
have), so that they will have to be changed, too. His marriage
with Line Form B is now consecrated, and he settles down to live
happily ever after. Then after a year or so, Wife B begins to prove
incompatible in a different and even more annoying way than
Wife A; and it occurs to him that if he could find some one who
had the best characteristics of both A and B, without their objec-
tionable traits, he could be truly happy. The editor is uniquely

privileged to be able to bring this dream-girl into existence by amalgamating A and B, which he does, and then weds this AxB after another expensive divorce. But the chances are that by now he is less illusioned about the excellence of his judgment in choosing wives, and while he likes his third one basically, he is prepared to expect that as time passes he may want to make a few changes in her. And at what time in his life will he be ready to say that he is fully and permanently satisfied with his choice? Never, until he stops thinking entirely.

This lack of decisiveness in an editor is surely a vice, but just as surely an inevitable one. For the determination of a right reading takes a very long time and is finally accomplished only after a number of minds have thought independently about the problem. A line of Chaucer's that I have recently discussed elsewhere has, I believe, been given in an unoriginal form in all editions but one of the *Canterbury Tales* from Caxton's first of 1478 through Professor Baugh's of 1964, as well as in all 52 of the surviving MSS. According to my version of the history of this line,[1] one wrong variant held sway for four centuries, only to be replaced by a wronger one, which lasted 61 years, which was succeeded in turn by another less wrong but still wrong, which has been challenged only once in the 25 years it has prevailed. What I am sure is the right reading of the line is suggested—not given—in only three MSS which are presumably 'bad'. Hence this reading has never been adopted except in my own edition. But persuaded as I am of my own rectitude, I am not foolish enough to expect the early triumph of a *lectio* that took almost half a millennium after the invention of printing to get itself into print: it must, of course, stand the test of even more time and the examination of minds less prejudiced than my own. At this rate Methuselah, provided he had taken up editing as a relatively young man, might live to know whether the readings he chose were the right ones. But those whose futures are numbered in decades or less may expect little certainty this side the grave.

Yet editors want to be right and want to be known to be right while they are still alive, not only because they are human (as, despite their own frequent efforts to disguise it, they are), but

---

[1] See my essay '*Canterbury Tales*, D117: A Critical Edition', reprinted below.

also because as scholars they are judged by their ability to be right. In such a situation, an editor is apt to heed a voice that whispers to him that the surest way of being right, or appearing to be, is to avoid the occasion of appearing to be wrong. In editorial activity, this results in the production of a conservative text, one that will hurt no feelings and will undoubtedly be treated kindly by reviewers. The psychology of reviewers of textual editions is not my topic, but I cannot help noting how dim a view many of them seem to take toward the whole business of editing, for they bestow the highest praise on purely negative achievements: 'Professor X has wisely refrained from emending for metrical reasons'. 'Dr Y has sensibly eschewed adopting readings from MS Q, tempting though some of them must have been to him'. Or, again, 'While his notes contain some interesting speculations, Mr Z has not disfigured his page with conjectural emendations'. One sometimes wonders whether the editor might not acquire the highest possible praise by refraining from doing anything at all, which would surely insure him against doing anything wrong. At any rate, remarks like these (which I have semi-fictionalized) set up in the mind of a future editor dire taboos, so that he may fail to ask himself what the special wisdom is in not emending for metrical reasons, or whether MS Q is really a scarlet whore rather than a chaste virgin, or whether Mr Z's interesting speculations may not represent his original author better than his undisfigured page does.

Actually, this habit which the reviewers have of praising negative achievements has always been encouraged by the editors theselves, who, historically, have suffered from a common psychic impulse. This, if it is not quite the death-wish, is akin to it: one might call it the wish for non-existence, or, at the very least, for invisibility. The editor is highly conscious—and if he isn't initially so, there is a vast literature to make him so—of the fact that he, a mere modern scholar, has arrogantly assumed a position where he will appear to be tampering with the works of some one of an old and very different culture and, frequently, of a totally different order of imagination from his own. In all likelihood his rest is constantly perturbed by the memory of such statements as the following, by Miss Hammond, discussing the proper method of choosing among variants in the Chaucer MSS:[2]

> ... No preconception [on the part of the editor] as to the probable truth must interfere; the scribes are called as witnesses, and the comparison of their testimony must be made independent of all attempts to interpret. Interpretation or exegesis comes later.
>
> Thus, if several varying versions of the same Chaucerian line ... are before the editor, he has no right to choose that one which seems to him likely in itself; if he does so, he is allowing a preconception to interfere, the preconception that his taste and Chaucer's must necessarily be in accord.

This is surely one of the most austerely idealistic statements of principle that was ever written: the editor is firmly ordered to keep the place that has been assigned him. The only trouble is that after twenty years of trying to edit various Middle English poems, I am entirely unclear what or where Miss Hammond believed the editor's place to be. Not only does her statement eliminate from the editorial process the editor's 'preconceptions', it also eliminates, as far as I can see, his learning, his judgment, his taste, his experience, and his intelligence: it reduces him not merely to invisibility, but to non-existence. I have sometimes tried to behave as Miss Hammond insists I should—sitting at my desk, judiciously writing down the testimony of the scribes and keeping all my preconceptions chained up. But I have always ended up with a mass of confusing testimony from the scribes, and no indication (from Miss Hammond) as to how I was to proceed from there, since to make any choice would be to suggest that I thought my taste and my author's were the same. The result was paralysis—non-existence of the editor and a non-edition of the author, though these non-results of my labours were, I had to admit, admirably objective.

I suppose I am being unfair to Miss Hammond, for she did actually allow some editorial functions to the editor, though not at the stage we have been discussing. She was talking in terms of editing by recension, which she still believed—despite what must have been a dispiriting experience with the *Parliament of Fowls*—to be a method by which one could achieve editorial

---

[2] E. P. Hammond, *Chaucer: A Bibliographical Manual* (New York, 1908), pp. 109–10.

objectivity. In recension, one's first task is, of course, to classify the MSS, and if one classifies them correctly, and if one is lucky enough to end up with a trifid stemma, three independent families, then one has some hope of producing what will appear to be an objective text. But I have always found it a curious dishonesty—or an unusual self-deception—on the part of those who claim that editing by recension is an objective process, that they say very little about the business of making the initial classification, which must be accomplished before editing itself begins. It is always carefully pointed out that MSS may be grouped together only on the basis of shared error, but it is seldom pointed out that if an editor has to be able to distinguish right readings from wrong in order to evolve a stemma which will in turn distinguish right readings from wrong *for* him, then he might as well go on using this God-given power to distinguish right from wrong throughout the whole editorial process, and eliminate the stemma. The only reason for not doing so is to eliminate the appearance—not the fact—of subjectivity: the fact remains that the whole classification depends on purely subjective choices made before the work of editing begins. It is as if the editor believed he had created a very complex machine, into which a god had made his way who could dictate to him the true text, and the editor must reverence the god; while in fact the voice is merely the echo of the editor's ancient preconceptions, the choices made so long ago that he has forgotten it was he who made them; the voice is his own, made to sound divine only through time and forgetfulness: *vox Dei, vox ed.* By becoming invisible even to himself, the editor thinks he has achieved non-existence.

This is a harsh condemnation of a widely-admired system, and I am sure that some one might like to point out that there is room for a very large measure of common sense in selecting errors of the kind that are necessary for classifying MSS—that is, that some errors are so obvious that their detection involves hardly any subjective judgment. This may be partly true, but it fails to get rid of at least two objections. The first depends on the fact that the chief claim for recension was that it was a 'scientific' method that virtually eliminated the frail human judgment from the editorial process. Yet if its first motion, the all-important one on which everything else depends, is in no way scientific, but a mere exercise of common sense, then the claim to be scientific is false. Furthermore, as I suggested a moment ago, if common sense provides the base on which everything else rests, then it is hard to see why common sense should not be the agency for getting everything else done. Otherwise, one seems to be in the peculiar position of saying in one's defence: 'Well, at any rate I have used as little common sense as I possibly could'.

The second objection to the classification of MSS on the basis of selected shared error is that it is based on a false premise. Miss Hammond, in her discussion of recension, states very clearly her belief that while all scribes introduce errors into their transcriptions, different scribes are unlikely to introduce the same errors. I shall return in a few minutes to what I suspect to have been the reasons for Miss Hammond's faith in a 'principle' which has since been shown to be false by Greg, Grattan, and others—most recently and most lucidly, by Professor Kane in the Introduction to his edition of the A-text of *Piers Plowman*.[1] For if there is one generalization that can safely be made about human beings, it is that, given the same circumstances, they make the same errors that others have made before them and will make after them, and the same errors that they themselves have made before and will make again. Since the Fall men keep on falling in the same old way. Any one who has taught spelling is aware that the same words are almost always misspelled in the same way, so that a pupil who misspells a word in a new way is almost as welcome to the bored teacher as a scribe who misunderstands a passage in a new way is to the jaundiced editor. As Professor Kane has noted, those crucial passages which on a glance seem most clearly to show MS affiliation on the basis of shared error are often the very ones that must be excluded from such consideration because the special difficulty of the context was bound to produce the same solutions in different scribes. This means, of course, that we are once more back in the realm of subjectivity, and in a double sense: before starting to edit, we must not only be able to distinguish right from wrong but we must further be able to distinguish between those wrongs that were probably inherited from a common ancestor and those

[1] G. Kane, *Piers Plowman: The A-Version* (London. 1960).

which might have come into being by coincidence. I do not believe that an editor who can make all these distinctions can pretend to be non-existent.

But how could it be that a 'principle' that seems now so patently false could have been proclaimed by a scholar so intelligent as Miss Hammond—and, despite the doubts cast by Bédier and Housman,[1] adhered to by hundreds of other respectable scholars? The answer, I believe, lies in the powerful charm that a totally mechanistic theory seems always to hold for scholars in the humanities. The genetic system of editing, as described by Miss Hammond and others, is an almost perfect machine. A fair text is brought into being by a medieval writer himself or by his scribe, whose work he supervised; this text is copied by several scribes—ideally three—who introduce a number of errors inadvertently (though, as we have noticed, they are apparently careful not to introduce the same errors as each other); their MSS are, in turn, copied by other scribes who introduce more errors of their own (while still avoiding each other's); centuries pass, the early MSS are lost; the editor assembles the relatively late remainders, analyzes them for shared error, finds that they fall into three independent families, is able to get a pretty clear notion of the three family archetypes, and then proceeds to edit according to the simple formula that with three independent families two against one is always decisive. Presto! The author's original text is restored, with what seems to have been a minimum of effort (or of thought) on the editor's part. No wonder he can remain invisible: all he has done is to reverse a machine, which, once reversed, operates as smoothly backward as before it did forward, and almost, as it were, on the same supply of fuel.

But what a false notion of human activity this ideal machine reflects! Take the very first point—the author's fair copy. It is safe to say that the number of writers who are capable of producing a fair copy of their own work themselves, or who are capable of correcting the errors in a fair copy of their own work made by some one else, without subjecting the whole thing to one more revision, is limited, to say the least (the recent rise in printers' wages may well have effected a great reform in the

[1] See below, p. 129, n. 1.

untidy habits of writers). Imaginative writers are probably more prone to reduce final fair copies to rough draughts than scholars, but I'm willing to wager that some of the reading-copies of the papers given at this conference are not legible by any one save their authors; and one has only to glance at Orm's MS of the *Ormulum* in the Bodleian to see what chaos can be produced by a mind that wants the final form to be just right. The result of this fact is that even if every other cog in the machine should work properly, the genetic editor might well end up with something little better than a mess as the author's original—though it seems implicit in the system as described that if the original is a mess, nothing on the lower level is going to work well.

The implied idea of operations on the lower level is even more false to the facts of humanity. The assumption is that the scribes who copy the work are themselves machines, though machines that have a kind of idealized faultiness built into them: all they ever do is make mistakes. Heaven forbid that instead of making mistakes they should correct the mistakes that they see in the exemplar from which they are copying, for if they do that, the whole machine breaks down. Instead of getting progressively worse, the text suddenly gets better, or it gets worse in a non-consecutive way. Innocently interested in the author's sense, not in some future editor's convenience, a scribe corrects a reading by glancing at a MS of a different family, or by searching his memory, or by simply using his intelligence. His reward for thus behaving in a scholarly rather than in a genetic way is that some day he will be referred to as an 'intelligent (i.e. meddlesome)' scribe, and his MS will be officially declared contaminated and unreliable. One can only hope that a scribe thus abused will be privileged to look in on the editor at the time he is considering a unique and uniquely good reading recovered somehow by the scribe: nothing on earth can equal the torment of a genetic editor facing the prospect of having to admire and perhaps introduce into his text a reading from a MS which could not possibly have come by it through honest inheritance: this is something that betrays both the editor's non-existence and his invisibility.

The not especially unhappy truth is that medieval scribes were not mere machines, but people, invariably human, though variously intelligent, and variously interested in what they were doing. And many of them seem to have had a normal human being's interest in getting things right even while they showed a normal human being's propensity for getting them wrong. A very large number of both the Chaucer and the Langland MSS have been corrected, either by the scribe himself or by some one else, and sometimes the corrections are very good (sometimes they are dreadful). It is by no means inconceivable that with any given medieval work some of the earliest MSS were heavily corrected, with the result that (in genetic terminology) whole families are contaminated that have hitherto been considered pure, a fact which would raise hob with the putative MS-relationships. If this is the case, then the scribes are having their revenge on the editors who have described them as mere machines. And it is a deserved revenge: I cannot help feeling that there is something basically wrong about a situation in which scholars, who are dedicated to upholding and fostering intelligence, can operate securely only if those who serve them— in this case scribes—are by definition stupid. Indeed, I should go so far as to suggest that any scholar who is alarmed by a show of intelligence four hundred years old deserves such invisibility and non-existence as he is able to achieve.

The final flaw in the beautiful machine is, of course, the lack of inevitability in arriving at the magic number three for the total of independent MS-families, so that the two-against-one formula may be employed. I have taken no census of genetic editions, and I have no statistics, but I should guess that three would come up no more reliably than two—though this is perhaps an area where the laws of probability have no application. Of course, if two comes up, the poor editor is left in the position of having nothing to hide behind: since there is no more genetic authority for Family A than for Family B, he will have constantly to choose between them on the basis of his preconceptions— though, as we shall see presently, he may be able to avoid such a dilemma by finding that one branch is, after all, more authoritative than the other, even if not on genetic grounds. It may seem contradictory to my belief in the editorial wish for non-existence that Bédier found, in a group of selected genetically-edited texts, that the editors generally managed to come up with two lines of descent, and even, at times when they came up with three, revised their stemma to get down to two. But I suspect, in disagreement with Bédier, that the editors were not so much voluntarily trying to escape from an intolerable prison of their own making, as being forced to face the fact that, even in the seemingly ideal situation of two-against-one, the two sometimes agreed in nonsense while the one was making sense—that for one reason or another the god in the machine was talking silly. This I do not find surprising in view of my dark suspicion that the two members were probably agreeing in coincident error. Bédier's shrewd observations surely point to two situations which must often have existed with editors and perhaps still do. In the first, the editor, having expended enormous labour on the erection of a stemma which has proved far less helpful than he had hoped, edits the poem with his left hand while with his right continually pointing to a stemma no one can possibly under-stand, thereby suggesting that a dynamic relationship really does exist. In the second, the editor quietly edits the poem and then revises his stemma to match his edition. This last is far less dishonest than it sounds—indeed, if I were to edit with care for genetic relationships, it is the method I should use. It is com-forting at least to know that what you think did happen textu-ally as a matter of fact could, according to your picture, have also happened genetically. I have a residual doubt, however, about the relevance of diagrams to the facts of life. An editor generally draws one, I suspect, to give himself the illusion that he has achieved some 'scientific' objectivity.

In making fun of the genetic system of editing, I have been kicking a dead horse, or a dying one—or, at least, I hope, a very ill one. I have done so because I am impressed by the fact that a system so obviously unrealistic could have long enjoyed the highest scholarly reputation, which suggests that it could happen again, especially when computers are exposing more and more of the charms that allure humanists: in a way, the genetic system was only a very primitive attempt to devise a computing mechanism that would do one's thinking for one. And I am depressed by the fact that it is still apparently a common scholarly feeling that editors ought to be invisible and should ideally be non-existent. Even the system of editing which has developed in recent years, though it avoids many of the absurdities of the genetic system, retains its ability to make the editor feel secure by remaining obscure. This system is best represented by Manly and Rickert's great edition of the *Canterbury Tales*. Here the editors did not try to classify MSS by shared error: instead, they collated against Skeat's 'Students' Edition' and hoped that the statistical abundance provided by the vast number of MSS and the vastness of the *Canterbury Tales* would get around the objection that shared right readings provide no evidence of affiliation. Moreover, they recognized the possibility of widespread contamination and allowed for it in every way they could, and resisted the temptation to consign contaminated MSS into outer darkness.[1] And finally, they allowed for the possibility that all the MSS descended from a single archetype which was not the author's perfectly proof-read autograph—a courtesy to which I shall return later.

Textually, the results seem fairly satisfactory—provided one remembers that their text is not intended to be what Chaucer wrote, but O^1, a copy with an unknown amount of deviation from what he wrote. Moreover the apparatus, which is gigantic, is amazingly accurate. One's principal objection is that even after one has read the entire second volume, mostly devoted to the classification of MSS, one hasn't got the foggiest notion of how they actually went about choosing any given reading. Yet at the same time, one is rarely led to suppose that any given reading was chosen on the simple grounds that it was the best reading: Manly and Rickert's most frequently used explanation is that their reading is that of the most authoritative MSS. By turning back to the second volume and rereading the section on classification, one does learn that certain MSS are considered more authoritative than others. But how do they earn this authority? Well, the answer seems to be, by avoidance of error —and we are back on the old merry-go-round. In the genetic system, I have always supposed that the illustory *vox Dei* got into the machine as a result of the time-lag between the editor's initial classification of the MSS and his ultimate editing of the text, but with Manly and Rickert I am never sure whether a given MS proved authoritative in volumes three and four

[1] M-R, ii, 5, 20–7.

(containing the text) and hence received the accolade in volume two, or whether its authority was predetermined in volume two and then allowed to express itself in volumes three and four. As I say, I have little quarrel with their text, and am willing to allow Hengwrt almost as much authority as they do. But I do object to the fact that Manly and Rickert never admit doing what they must have been constantly doing—judging readings with all their quite considerable preconceptions (i.e. their learning, taste, and judgment) and then making their free choice. I object to the fact that they constantly seem to be taking refuge in the idea of an apparently predetermined 'authoritative' MS, and pretending it has an authority which they don't.

For the fact is that a MS has only that authority which an editor is willing to concede it. This proposition is perhaps clearer on the negative side than it is on the positive. A manuscript which is said to lack authority is so described because it gives a large number of bad readings. It follows that a MS that is frequently wrong obviously should not be trusted, while one that is generally right should be trusted. But there is a fallacy here for, theoretically, if the editor knows the difference between a good reading and a bad one, he does not have to trust any MS: he can trust his own judgment. After he has finished editing, he can compare his own text with the MSS and find out which of them most nearly resembles it, and declare that to be the most authoritative—though it will no longer matter. Practically, of course, the concept of the 'authoritative' MS has several uses. The first is, if a MS reads right on a great many occasions where the editor can tell right from wrong, then there is a presumption in favour of its being right in the cases where he cannot tell right from wrong. And, as a partial inference from this, when the editor is challenged on a reading derived from the authoritative MS, he can always point to the MS as the authority—and once more invisibility descends upon him, which he can readily convert to non-existence by constantly sticking to the authoritative MS— as Housman said, like Hope to her anchor—and then ascribing his behaviour to the authoritativeness of the MS.

Now in any test there are, to be sure, many places where it is impossible for any editor to decide which of two equally good and equally trivial variants is original. If he is using a MS as his base, these instances are covered by Greg's rule of copy-text; if, like Manly and Rickert, he has no base, then the doctrine of the authoritative MS should apply: it has been found faithful in great matters, let it be trusted in small. But there are also some relatively important places where the editor may be unable to decide between variants. For instance, in the Physician's-Pardoner's Link, the Host, when he calls upon the Pardoner, addresses him, in the standard texts, as 'Thow beel amy, thow. Pardoner', but in an impressive array of MSS he says, 'Thow beel amy, John Pardoner'. The only conceivable reason for preferring *thow* to *John* is the fact that some of the 'best' MSS, including Ellesmere and Hengwrt, have *thow*. But, despite their universally accepted authority, the 'best' MSS, including Ellesmere and Hengwrt, are wrong in their readings on many occasions, where all editors have unhesitatingly emended them. The truth is that a MS's authority extends no farther than any line in which it is known to be right: in any line where the editor cannot determine the reading it may well be wrong, and some supposedly 'inferior' MS may be right—as, in the line whose history I outlined a while ago, only three very 'bad' MSS preserve the correct word. I labour this point, because readers of editions are apt to be easily taken in by editorial rhetoric on the subject of MSS (once more, I fictionalize slightly): 'A splendid MS, written in a neat hand on vellum in a good London spelling; probably first quarter of 14C; highly authoritative'. 'A rather sloppy MS, written in a poor hand on paper, probably in Norfolk; much gnawed by rats; after 1450; of no authority'. It is obvious that in one case the London scribe's neat hand on vellum is being made to contribute to the impression of reliability, while in the other the rats ably support the editor's bad opinion of the non-calligraphic provincial. You may be sure that if an Ellesmere had suffered similarly, editors would have enlisted the reader's sympathy by writing, 'unfortunately damaged by vermin'. With such devices editors build up the authority of authoritative MSS, so that when they themselves cannot determine the original reading, they give the impression that they have left the matter in better hands than their own. Now while I sympathize with an editor who follows a MS he is fond of when all other resources fail him (as indeed I did myself in the matter of *thow* and *John*), I do not think he should imply that this is an admirable course—he should not be permitted to make a virtue of his necessity. And he should certainly not be permitted to use the authority of a MS instead of his own head. Perhaps we ought to devise a new symbol, to be placed prominently in the text when authority is being docilely followed, one that means, 'Editor has no idea what to read here, and hence is taking refuge, as usual, in dear old MS Pf'. A small ostrich, with head in the sand, might do.

I hope it is clear that Manly and Rickert are not the butt of all my disagreeable remarks—only of those having to do with the cult of the 'more authoritative' MS. I fear in this they set a fashion, for I have observed in several recent editions influenced by theirs a tendency to exalt one MS into a supreme position, often by a simple assertion; for instance, from a reading text in Middle English: 'I have followed X, which is generally agreed to be the most authoritative MS, and only emended it where its sense was seriously deficient'. That is, he has refrained from editing except where the text rose up and howled at him; he has attained what is logically the penultimate stage of the editorial wish for non-existence—the stage where the editor does not even claim to edit; he just transcribes. The ultimate stage is, of course, the camera.

Manly and Rickert were, in most respects, the most scrupulous of editors, even going so far as to place an asterisk before the apparatus of any line in which they were uncertain of the reading. And this brings us to a matter that is related to the psychology of editors: the psychology of users of editions. As a reader of Manly and Rickert, I find myself constantly forgetting to heed their asterisks: for instance I do not know now whether the *thow/John* alternate is provided with an asterisk or not, though I recall their—unfortunately quite reversible—argument for *thow*.[1] And I believe I am not alone in my failure to heed the asterisk, for I have several times noticed competent scholars citing a line from Manly and Rickert as if there were no possible doubt about it although it is dutifully prefixed with an asterisk.

---

[1] The line is indeed prefixed with an asterisk: M–R, iv, 81. But the critical note's suggestion (iv, 492) that *Ihon* 'originated in a hasty reading of' *thou* neglects the fact that *thou* could similarly originate from *Ihon*.

The fault is, to be sure, partly the editors', who not infrequently make an elaborate defence of the reading they have chosen, even though the asterisk presumably means that they do not entirely believe their own defence. Nevertheless, a rigorous reading of the edition would relieve them of the responsibility for having been 'authoritative' when they did not really mean to be so. But rigorous readings of editions are rare: take the simple matter of the Manly-Rickert text itself, which, as I have said, is not intended exactly to represent what Chaucer wrote, but represents something which lies removed from it an unknown distance: this fact is made clear—though I must admit it is not made very clear—in Volume II. Yet after twenty-five years the Manly-Rickert text is capable of misleading readers into supposing it to be something better than it claims to be, and editors of Chaucer occasionally follow Manly and Rickert in readings which, in their critical notes, Manly and Rickert specifically label unChaucerian. Even so canny a scholar as Mr Bateson implies in his recent guide to English Literature that the Manly and Rickert text shows Chaucer's metre to have been less regular than earlier editions have made it seem.[1] But this is not true (even though Manly himself seems to have believed it was), unless it can be proved that O^1 preserves all the metrical features of Chaucer's own MS—which I don't know that any one has tried to prove. Let me add that to misunderstand Manly and Rickert's intention is easily forgivable, not only because of the obscurity of their statement of it, but also because, I suspect, they sometimes themselves forgot the difference between O and O^1— though they remembered it often enough to write some critical notes in which they conjecture what the original reading must have been.

Yet the example of the Manly and Rickert edition shows clearly that, notwithstanding disclaimers by the editor, even scholarly readers will believe that what is printed in the text represents what in the editor's best judgment he believes the author wrote. I do not think that editors should be allowed to exploit this very human failing so that they can have it both ways—the impression of authority in the text, the impression of admirable scholarly circumspection in the notes, or *vice versa*.

[1] F. W. Bateson, *A Guide to English Literature* (London, 1965), p. 24.

They should surely not be allowed to do what the editor of a late Middle English text has recently done—tell us in the notes how the text should, but does not, read. Few are going to examine his notes; and of those who do almost no one is going to believe that his notes take priority over his text—for if the editor really thought the text read that way, why in the world didn't he print it that way? This situation seems to me to impose on an editor the responsibility to print, in his text, where no one can miss it, the reading he considers right.

Of course if the injunction is taken in the deeper sense of what 'he considers right'—and that is how I really mean it—then the editor will have to exercise his judgment and to make, honestly, the best decision he is capable of about every line before he prints it. And this will require using all his preconceptions—his learning, his taste, his experience, his judgment, his wisdom—and accepting that responsibility for what he does which has always been his. If he behaves this way, he will, of course, no longer be able to hide among the bushy branches of his MSS' family tree or behind the vellum skirts of that neat London MS: he will be revealed in all his nakedness, just where the taboos say he shouldn't be, not merely interfering, but positively obtruding himself, between the reader and the author. And when the reviews start appearing, his wish for invisibility or non-existence may well become a full-grown death-wish.

But there will be compensations—for scholarship, if not for the editor. We must by now owe it to the reviewers to give them something to do besides praise us for our negative achievements: let us stimulate them into damning us roundly for our shameless behaviour. And, while they're on the subject, let them tell us why—and in detail—we shouldn't have emended for metrical reasons, or shouldn't have yielded to the tempting readings of MS Q, or why conjectural emendations may be properly said to disfigure a page. In short, let us provoke them—and our readers, and ourselves—to thought, which is the purest of scholarly pleasures; and I address this exhortation perhaps more to myself than to anyone else. If we do this, we shall surely cause heat; but we shall achieve, I hope, more light.

8

CANTERBURY TALES, D117:
A CRITICAL EDITION

> Telle me also to what conclusioun
> Were membres maad of generacioun
> And of so parfit wys a wight ywroght?

THUS the Wife of Bath's embarrassing question as it appears in Manly and Rickert.[1] Immediately below I list the last of the three lines (D117) in six different forms derived from the 52 MSS that testify to the line's existence. I hope, by analysis of the problems created by the variant forms of a single line, to suggest what some of the responsibilities—and pleasures—of an editor of Middle English poetry are—or should be. It may well seem to some readers that I am confusing pleasure with pedantry; nevertheless, I also hope that those readers who like bridge problems will enjoy playing out the hand dealt by the 52 MSS.

1. And of so parfit $\frac{\text{wys (Hg)}}{\text{wise (Dd)}}$ a wight ywroght

   Thus HgDdAd¹Bo²ChCnEn¹En³HkHtMaRa³Tc¹Tc² *and, with vv.,* Ad³DsHa⁵NePs: of) *om* Ad³Ds. so) *om* Ha⁵Ps. wys) *vice* Ne. wight) wight is Ps.

2. And of so parfit and wys a wight ywroght
   Thus McRa¹.

3. And of so parfit wise and why ywroght
   Thus CpDlFiGlHa²LaLd¹MmPh³PwRy¹Sl²To *and, with vv.,* BwIiLcMgNlPySeSl¹: of) in BwPySe; *om* LcMg. and why) and how Sl¹; that were Bw; a thyng Py; were Nl; *om* Ii.

4. And in what wise was a wight ywroght
   Thus Ha⁴Ra².

---

[1] *The Text of the Canterbury Tales,* iii, 240. My information is derived from M–R (especially vi, 15, where the variants of D117 are given) and from the Chaucer Society's Six-Text (CpElGgHgLaPw) plus the two supplementary volumes (DdHa⁴), ed. F. J. Furnivall (1868–1903).

5. And for what profit was a wight ywroght
   Thus ElBo¹Ph² *and, with vv.*, GgSi: profit) parfit Si. wight) wyf Gg.
6. And of so parfit wys a wrighte ywroght
   Thus no MS, *but cf.*: And so parfit wys (wise?) a wrighte ywroght
   Ld²Ry²; And so parfit and so wys a wrighte it wroghte Ln.

Note 1: Information is lacking on the distribution of the spellings *wys* and *wise*: in **1**, as noted, Hg has *wys*, Dd has *wise*; in **3** CpLaPw have *wise*; in **4** Ha⁴ has *wise*. Actual spellings for all other MSS are unavailable. The spelling of other words has been normalized on the HgEl model.

Note 2: The source of the passage is acknowledged to be St Jerome, *Epistola adversus Jovinianum*, Migne, PL xxiii, col. 260: 'Et cur, inquies, creata sunt genitalia, et sic a conditore sapientissimo fabricati sumus, ut mutuum nostri patiamur ardorem, et gestiamus in naturalem copulam?'

Form **1** is represented with approximate fidelity by 19 MSS: this is the way the line appears—with Hengwrt's spelling *wys*— not only in Manly and Rickert, but also in Robinson's second edition and in Professor Baugh's recent text.[1] It is also the way the line appears—though with the Dd spelling *wise*—in the great majority of editions printed from Caxton's first in 1478 through Skeat's revision of Bell in 1878.[2] Form **2** appears only in two closely related MSS, one of them probably a copy of the other,[3] and in no printed text. Form **3** occurs, with some rather wide variation, in 21 MSS, and has been preferred by two editors, Urry in 1721 and Morris in 1866.[4] Form **4** occurs in only two MSS

[1] Robinson, p. 77 (1st ed., 1933); A. C. Baugh, *Chaucer's Major Poetry* (New York, 1963), p. 384.

[2] Listed here in short form are the chief editions of Chaucer containing D117 printed before 1940 that I have seen: Caxton 1478, 1484; Pynson 1490, 1526; de Worde 1498; Thynne 1532, 1542, etc.; Stow 1561; Speght 1598, 1602, 1687; Urry 1721; Tyrwhitt 1775–78 (reprinted many times, including John Bell 1782, Anderson 1793–1795, Chalmers 1810, 'Aldine' 1845); Thomas Wright 1847–51 (reprinted several times); Robert Bell 1854–56; Richard Morris's 1866 revision of 'Aldine' (reprinted as late as 1906); W. W. Skeat's 1878 revision of Robert Bell; Arthur Gilman 1879; Skeat's *Oxford* edition 1894; A. W. Pollard 1894; 'Kelmscott' 1896; Pollard *et al.* *Globe* 1898; John Koch 1915; Robinson 1st ed. 1933. All editions up to Gilman, except Urry and Morris, read with Dd. Many minor nineteenth-century printings fail to mention the source of their text, which seems generally to have been Tyrwhitt's. In the earlier years of this century the Wife of Bath's Prologue—or at least the present passage—was commonly omitted from students' editions.

[3] M–R, i, 357.

[4] This reading also appears in the Everyman version of Arthur Burrell (1906), which, however, hardly enjoys the status of an edition.

and has never been elected. Form **5** occurs in five MSS including Ellesmere, on the authority of which it was adopted by Gilman in 1879, by Skeat in the *Oxford* Chaucer of 1894, by Pollard and the *Globe* editors, by Koch, by Robinson in his first edition, and, I believe, by all other editors who had the good courage to print the passage between 1879 and 1940, when the great Manly and Rickert text was published. Form **6** occurs in no MS, though something suggesting it occurs in three related MSS, one of which, Ld², is here probably a copy of another, Ry². Thus frailly supported, Form **6** has been adopted by only one—rash—editor.[1]

In thus discussing the editorial history of a line, without first worrying about its meaning—as though it were a dry bone into which no life could ever come again—I have been guilty of the worst of editorial bad habits: before thinking about meaning, always examine the credentials of the agents by which meaning is communicated. This bad habit explains why many of us were brought up to believe what Form **5**, the Ellesmere variant, tells us: that the Wife of Bath considered sexual intercourse the whole purpose of mortal existence, or else, for what profit *was* a person created? I am sure that Chaucer never intended us to believe this. The reason we did so is that Ellesmere is a splendid MS, which, in hundreds of cases where the majority gives a rough reading, gives a smooth one. Moreover, it is grammatical, legible, and illustrated. Its great virtue was recognized as soon as Furnivall began printing it in the Chaucer Society's Six-Text in 1868, and within eleven years it came to be regarded as the answer to any editor's prayer. For the next sixty-one years all new editions reproduced its version of D117: a characteristically clean and clear reading that stands in sharp contrast with the murky uncertainty of the majority.

An editor is surely fortunate to have at his hand a 'correct' MS like Ellesmere to which he can turn when all else fails: that is, on the many occasions when he is faced by several variant readings, no one of which may be judged superior to the others by any possible operation of editorial perspicuity. But the danger in having so helpful a friend-in-need is that one comes to rely on him when there isn't any need—or rather, when the need is

[1] *Chaucer's Poetry*, p. 154. For the relation of the three MSS, see M–R, i, 316, 331, 487.

to think, to reject the easy answer until all the hard ones have been examined and found wanting. When an editor relies too much on a MS, he becomes its servant, taking its dictation and forgetting that it was himself who first invested it with authority. Moreover, the investment was necessarily made on incomplete evidence, so that he ought properly to test its validity whenever the possibility of a test offers itself. Integrity asks that no editor accept the reading of any MS, however authoritatively it has behaved before, unless he is satisfied that its reading could somehow have given rise to the other variants—or at least that it is unlikely that the other variants gave rise to it.

In the present case we ought to ask how, if Form 5 was the original, the other five forms of the line, which resemble each other more than they do 5, could have arisen from it? The trouble with 5 is that it is so marvellously plausible: it says exactly what every schoolboy wants the Wife of Bath to be saying at this point, and if Chaucer had had her say it, few scribes would have quarrelled with him (as, for a long time, no editor did), and surely not in the variety of ways illustrated; those who did want to quarrel would probably have hit upon a solution like Gg's (see 5): 'And for what profit was a wyf ywroght'. This at least centres the generalization on the Wife of Bath herself, rather than on the whole human race. Yet Ellesmere suggests that she thinks that every one ought to share her own preoccupation with sexual play, even though throughout her Prologue she shows full awareness of her own idiosyncrasy in this regard. The race of the chaste is still run, though she is only a spectator; she is content to be a wooden vessel in the Lord's household, without prejudice to gold and silver—to be barley bread without prejudice to wheat. She will exercise her special talent—her *propre yifte*— while allowing others to exercise their different ones.[1] It is true that Alice is not entirely consistent on every subject; but on this point, except in Ellesmere and its relatives, she is. If we had only Ellesmere here, we should have to swallow a gross inconsistency; and because for a long time Ellesmere was all we did have, I believe that many readers found in the Wife of Bath a grossness that Chaucer never meant her to have.

[1] See D75-6, 95-104, 142-6.

But if Ellesmere is wrong, how did it evolve from the pattern represented by the other variants? The obvious palaeographic explanation, suggested by Manly and Rickert's note,[1] is of no help in establishing priority. While it is true that *parfit* is easily mistaken for *profit* because of the similarity of the abbreviations for *par (per)* and *pro*, it is equally true that *profit* is easily mistaken for *parfit*: in Form **5**, Si reads, 'And for what parfit was a wight ywroght', though its exemplar probably read *profit*. Since palaeographical explanations generally work equally well either way, it is sense that must determine the original form of a line.

Turning to Variants **1**, **2**, **3**, **4**, and **6**, one may discern three principal areas of scribal uncertainty. The preposition at the beginning of the line is generally *of*, but sometimes *in*, and is sometimes omitted; the words before the past participle at the end of the line appear as *a wight*, *a wrighte*, and *and why*, as well as showing other alternatives, including omission. But the hardest to deal with, and the one that most of the others probably depend on, is the alternation in the middle of the line: is the word *wys* as in the Hengwrt version of **1**, or is it *wise* as in the Dd version? In Hengwrt, which is one of the oldest MSS and preserves good fourteenth-century grammar,[2] the word must be an adjective, because in Chaucer's language the adjective meaning 'wise' is spelled without final *e* when it stands in the strong position, as it does here. On the other hand, the noun *wise*, 'manner, fashion', an Old English feminine, always has the final *e* in Chaucer: thus in Variants **3** and **4**, the spelling of Cp and Ha⁴ is correct, for the context requires the noun. Similarly, in **1** the spelling of Dd, *wise*, might also be taken to indicate that the scribe read the noun. But here, of course, the context is ambiguous, and we cannot be sure of the intention. For in the fifteenth century when final *e* became silent its old grammatical function was replaced by an orthographic one, and *e* was added to words, especially monosyllables, to indicate an antecedent long vowel. Thus in all positions the adjective meaning 'wise' was spelled *wise*, and noun and adjective became the homographs they now are. MS Dd is a little younger than Hengwrt, and slightly less grammatical, sometimes using *e* to indicate length.[3] But in the present case, the scribe of Dd probably meant a noun: in

[1] M–R, iii, 455. [2] M–R, i, 276, 151. [3] M–R, i, 102.

Hengwrt, the mark for the caesura is at the end of the line, for there is no place within the line where one may pause if one reads *wys* as an adjective: 'And of so perfectly wise a wight wrought?' But in Dd the mark occurs after *wise*, which is logical only if *wise* is considered a noun: 'And of so perfect wise / a wight wrought'.[1]

As I explain above in Note 1 to the listening of variants, I have only a few of the actual MS-spellings of the crucial word. I apologize for this, but point out that even if we had the spellings we could infer little from them. After the first quarter of the fifteenth century the adjective was very commonly spelled like the noun, and of the MSS in 1, apart from Hg (1400–10) and Dd (1400–20), only Bo² and En¹ could be as early as 1430, while the majority are of the mid-century, so that any spelling *wise* would be ambiguous.[2] In 2, of course, regardless of how the word is spelled, the adjective is meant. Here the scribe has done what scribes sometimes do when confronted with ambiguity: he has made clear what he thought was right by the most economical sort of operation—the insertion of a colourless conjunction without regard for the metre. In 3 and 4, on the other hand, scribes made up their minds in the opposite direction, selecting the noun *wise*. Furthermore, there are two MSS in 1 which also show that they read the noun. These are Ad³ and Ds, which omit the preposition. If one reads the line with the adjective, as in Hengwrt, the preposition is essential in order to make sense: *of* used in the old agent function governing *wight* and meaning 'by':[3] 'wrought by so perfectly wise a wight'. But in adverbial expressions of manner, the noun *wise* may be used without any preposition if it is modified by an adjective: 'and so perfect-wise a wight created'.[4] Thus in 3 also several MSS omit the preposition with noun *wise*, while others, as in 4, substitute *in* for *of*.

If one assumes, with Manly and Rickert, that Form 1 in the Hengwrt spelling is the archetypal reading from which all other variants derive, one may, I think, be at least momentarily surprised at the range of variation it produced. Scribes usually

---

[1] See the Chaucer Society printings.

[2] For dates of MSS, see M–R, ii, 46–8. Since the noun is rarely if ever spelled *wys*, any MS in 1 using this spelling would provide support for Hg's reading.

[3] See *OED*, *of*, prep., v, 15.   [4] See *OED*, *wise*, sb.¹, ii, *passim*.

bother to eliminate potential ambiguity only when it can be done with a minimum of effort. Thus, if a well-trained scribe recognized the adjective *wys* but rejected it as non-auctorial, he would normally add a final *e* and read the noun as Dd does; or if he felt the adjective was so important that no reader should possibly miss it, he could do what the MSS in 2 do. But Forms 3, 4, and 5 share an unusual radicalism: not only do they reject the sense produced by the adjective *wys*, they write the line in such a way as to prevent the reader from ever being able to understand that sense. In 3 and 4 the interpretation of *wise* as a noun has been insured by the elimination or alteration of other words of relatively heavy semantic value; and in 5 the potentially ambiguous word has been entirely replaced. In 5 a case could be made for palaeographic misunderstanding; but the range of variations represented by 5 along with 4 and 3 looks more like the result of conscientious editorial activity than of scribal blundering. It is not that any words in the archetype were very hard: it was, apparently, that they were simply incredible. Many fifteenth-century scribes could not believe that Chaucer had written that generative organs were created by a perfectly wise person. This is what Hengwrt tells us; it is how in Robinson's second edition the glossary causes the line to be read, and how Professor Baugh glosses it, translating the phrase of *so parfit wys a wight ywroght* as 'by so perfectly wise a person'.[1] But I hope, as he wrote the words, he was careful to do what John the carpenter did for Nicholas in the Miller's Tale: to *crouche* himself *from elves and fro wightes*. For while wights are indeed persons, and may also be spooky critters, the Creator is not a wight. For all her heterodoxy, Alice of Bath is never impious. She treats men with fine disrespect, but in her dealings with the Almighty she is scrupulously orthodox, and she calls Him by His accepted names. And, so far as I can discover, if she had called Him a wight, she would have been the only person in Old or Middle English ever to do so.[2] To be called a wight, a creature, is, indeed, the

[1] loc. cit.
[2] No use of *wight*, sb., as applied to the deity is listed in *OED*. But the term may be applied to the third person of the Trinity in the 'creatural' sense; thus, as Professor A. K. Hieatt has pointed out to me, in the *Second Shepherds' Play*, l. 709, one of the shepherds calls upon the Lord for 'somkyns gle' to comfort His 'wight'—the Christ-child.

only thing that is impossible to the Creator in medieval England.

In D117 of the *Canterbury Tales* what drove the scribes to such variation was their reluctance to transcribe this extraordinary epithet. The line in the archetype of most—perhaps all—of the extant MSS must have read as it does in Hengwrt, and Manly and Rickert were entirely right to choose it for their text. Indeed, it is a splendid example of a *durior lectio*, since its hardness of sense (not of words) explains all but one of the other variations. Its sense is truly puzzling. But I think if the reader will study **3** and **4** he will find their several senses also unsatisfactory (I hope my earlier remarks have pointed out the weakness of **5**). As a matter of fact, in the first five line forms the best sense is that of **1** in the Dd spelling: 'And of so perfect manner a person created'. Apparently this is how Pynson understood the line, for in his 1526 edition he placed a caesural mark after the word *wise* in the manner of Dd, and I suppose that other early editors made the same interpretation. Furthermore, a number of modern text book editors, while spelling *wys* after Manly and Rickert or Robinson's second edition, gloss the word as meaning 'manner'[1] —an incorrect but nevertheless understandable procedure.

As a matter of fact, it is doubly incorrect. I pointed out earlier that in the Hengwrt line the preposition *of* must mean 'by' and govern the noun *wight*, and that scribes who read *wise*, 'manner', sometimes either omitted the preposition (see in **1** Ad³Ds and in **3** LcMg) or altered it to *in* (see in **3** BwPySe and both MSS in **4**). What might seem surprising is that more of them did not edit the preposition, for elsewhere in Chaucer's work there is no such adverbial expression as '(performed) *of* such a wise'. In about two hundred and twenty adverbial expressions of manner with the noun *wise* listed in Tatlock's *Concordance* Chaucer either writes '*in* such a wise' (rarely *on*) or omits the preposition, though of course he writes *of* when the phrase is adjectival: 'With alle the rites of his payen wise' (A2370). And Chaucer was merely writing English as it has been spoken since

[1] Thus C. W. Dunn in *Major British Writers* (New York, 1954), i, 45; Daniel Cook, *The Canterbury Tales* (Garden City, 1961), and A. C. Cawley, *The Canterbury Tales*, Everyman (London, 1958), p. 161.

the Conquest: the *Oxford Dictionary* lists no example of adverbial
'of such a wise' since Old English times, and it was rare
then.[1] Thus the phrase 'of so perfect a fashion created' is a syntactical improbability. In Form 3 it is possible that the majority
reading *of* is intended to be adjectival, modifying *membres* in the
preceding line, but I suspect that most scribes were not troubled
by the preposition, assuming it was an archaism: there was
much change in prepositional usage in their century. But the
occurrence of the preposition *of* used anomalously in an adverbial
expression of manner is strong proof that the archetype read the
adjective *wys*, for if Chaucer had intended the noun *wise* he
would have written the preposition *in*; and if he had written *in*,
no one would have substituted for it a meaningless *of*, and there
would have been no crux. 'And *in* so parfit wise a wight
ywroght' is good syntax and makes good sense that even has
some support from St Jerome.[2]

Yet the more original reading is not this, but Hengwrt's, which
is only two letters away from what Chaucer must have written.
By now the reader will have put the quotation from St Jerome
(given in Note 2 to the listing of variants) together with Form 6.
In this part of her discourse, the Wife of Bath is following
St Jerome very closely, if in her own wayward way, and I see no
reason for her to avoid using his term for the Creator: for Latin
conditor, 'maker', is exactly translated by Middle English
wrighte, 'maker', which is the direct descendant of Old English
wyrhta, 'maker', and the English term was used as an epithet for
the Creator as late as 1300.[3] In the *Piers Plowman* MSS *wrighte* is
several times scribally reduced to *wight*,[4] and this is the reduction

---

[1] Both *OED*, *wise*, sb.,[1] ii, 2a, and Bosworth-Toller list but one example of the
phrase *of þisse wisan*—from Blickling Homilies, 31.16, where the sense is not entirely
clear; no other example is given in the *OED* article *of*, prep.

[2] Thus St Jerome (see Note 2 to the listing of variants, above) hazily remembered
(*e.g.*, 'cur . . . [tam] sapientissim[e] fabricati sumus') might yield the sense under
discussion.

[3] *OED*, *wright*, sb.,[1] 1b, cites *Cursor Mundi* for the latest use of the word applied
to the Creator.

[4] At B x. 401 MS Cot reads *wyghtte* for *wright*, as do OC[2] at B xi. 340, where R reads
wit: at B x. 404 WHmCr read *wightes* for *wrightes*. In two other uses of the word,
Chaucer was luckier: in A614 his phrasing, 'a wel good wrighte, a carpenter',
insured retention of the correct form, and at A3143 only four MSS reject *wrightes*,
three of them substituting the gloss *carpenteres*, and the fourth rewriting; if,

that some scribe early in the transmission of the *Canterbury Tales* must inadvertently have made of Alice's old-fashioned term.

Unfortunately *wrighte* appears in only three of the 52 MSS and in two of these, the twins Ld²Ry², it fails to make much sense whether one reads the adjective *wys* or the noun *wise*. MS Ln makes good sense, but only with the visible aid of a corrector who destroys both metre and rhyme, for the preterite *wroghte* with final *e* fails to rhyme with *e*-less *noght* in the next line. Furthermore, Manly and Rickert tell us that these MSS have no textual authority whatsoever.[1] It is little wonder that editors have refused to take them seriously in this line.

Yet we must remember that when Manly and Rickert say 'authority', they mean authority for O¹, that corrupt, or at least imperfect, archetype that was not Chaucer's autograph but was presumably the ancestor of all extant MSS.[2] They might well argue here that the three MSS came by the word *wrighte* dishonestly—that it was introduced by correction at a late stage in the transmission, and hence of no authority in determining O¹. Nor would I necessarily argue against such a hypothesis; but I will argue for the right and the responsibility of an editor who is trying to reconstruct Chaucer's text—not merely O¹—to let all MSS help him, not just the respectable ones.[3] Earlier, in the case of the Ellesmere variant, we saw how the idea of a 'good' MS may tyrannize over the editorial process; in the present case we see how the idea of a 'bad' MS does the same. Since Ld²Ry²Ln are bad MSS, it follows that they cannot help us. Now when we say 'good' and 'bad' we seem inevitably to connote moral values, and many editors refer to MSS as though they were good or bad citizens. Yet a MS has no moral nature: in any one line it is merely a tool which is helpful or not helpful. Since poems

however, Chaucer originally wrote *wrighte* in *House of Fame* 919 (2.411) three of five witnesses (BFTh) and most editors except *Globe* have preferred *wrecche*.

[1] See M–R, i, 317, 331, 487.

[2] I am under the impression that many users of M–R sometimes forget the distinction between O¹ and Chaucer's original text: see the discussion above, pp. 116–17.

[3] Manly and Rickert themselves uphold this point—though not so often as one might wish: see their note to B3479 (iv, 510), where they argue for the originality of a reading 'found in only two MSS and those usually lightly regarded'.

consist of a series of single lines, the degree of any MS's helpful-
ness may vary widely, and in line D117 three normally 'bad'
MSS are uniquely helpful. Nor need an editor worry that a MS
may have got its helpful reading dishonestly. We don't have to
write character references for MSS: we just have to use them.

During the last century hope burgeoned that a scientific
system might be devised that would make it possible to reconstruct old texts without the kind of special pleading represented by this article. The result of this hope was that, despite
protests like Bédier's and Housman's,[1] editors put more and
more energy into devising the system, and less and less into
studying the text, until all editorial resources tended to be reduced to one: classification of MSS, that vast machine which
would eliminate all human bias. This noble ideal failed to produce texts of the quality expected from it, partly because instead of eliminating bias, it built it into the machine as a hidden
component; but more because it made people who should have
been behaving like editors intent on the analysis of meaning
behave like mechanics tinkering with machines. It always sad-
dens me to contemplate the enormous energy that Manly and
Rickert devoted to classification of MSS, especially when I sometimes suspect that their choice in any given line—the present
one, for instance[2]—was less a result of an unequivocal mandate
from their system than of the simple assertion of their own
sound learning and sound sense. And sense and learning, not
machines—even computing machines—are a scholar's chief
resources.

It takes a very long time to establish a reading: a half an hour
of the reader's time for me to try to get two letters back into a
single line of Chaucer, five and a half centuries to arrive at the
attempt, and probably another century to find out if the attempt

---

[1] See A. E. Housman, *Selected Prose*, ed. John Carter (Cambridge, 1961) for ample
selections from the Preface to Manilius (1903), the Preface to Juvenal (1905), and the
whole of 'The Application of Thought to Textual Criticism', originally in *Proceedings
of the Classical Association*, xviii (1922). Joseph Bédier's position is summed up in
La Tradition manuscrite du Lai de l'ombre (Paris, 1929).

[2] Manly and Rickert never explained clearly how their classificatory system dic-
tated readings: one has to infer it from their lengthy discussions. I confess that when
I compare their classification of MSS for the Wife of Bath's Prologue (vi, 2) with the
variants for D117 no one reading impresses me as inevitable.

was worth making. Perhaps if we would concentrate harder on the text, the process could be speeded up.[1]

---

[1] In his recent *Selections from the Tales of Canterbury and Short Poems* (Boston: Houghton Mifflin, 1966), Robert A. Pratt reads *wight* in D117 and glosses as 'person', referring for support to B¹476, '[Who saved Daniel, etc. ?] No wight but God', and to D493, 'Ther was no wight save God and he that wiste'. But it is obvious that in these cases God is only accidentally and inferentially classed as a *wight* through the inevitable anthropomorphism of idiomatic speech, which lacks a common word for a class of being that would include both God and man.

9

THE MILLER'S TALE, A 3483-6

Jhesu Crist and seinte Benedight,
Blesse this hous from every wikked wight,
For nyghtes verye, the white *pater-noster*!
Where wentestow, seinte Petres soster?

MANLY AND RICKERT observe that until this 'charm is better
understood we cannot be sure of several words, as the scribes
were obviously puzzled'.[1] It is of course possible that John the
carpenter had no idea what his charm meant, and even that
Chaucer wasn't entirely sure either: it was only important that
the guardian spirits should understand. Therefore I trust it
would in no way offend them to suggest, in trying to rescue one
of the charm's words from scribal and talismanic obscurity, that
the spirits understood Old English.

The third line contains a word that has been printed by Robinson (see above), by Skeat, and by the *Globe* editors, as *verye*, but
by Koch and by Manly and Rickert as *uerye*.[2] The meaning of the
word is uncertain: Skeat suggested that *for nyghtes verye* might
represent OE *for nihte werigum*, 'against the evil spirits of the
night'; and Thoms sought to connect *verye* with *Wera, Werre*,
the name of a witch in German legend.[3] In either case, however,
a difficulty is raised by the interchange of *v* and *w*, which, while
common in Scotland, is unlikely in either Chaucer's or John's
dialect.[4] Another possibility is suggested by the reading of the
MSS followed by Koch and by Manly and Rickert. While the
great majority read *verye* and a few others have the eccentric
forms *verray, varie, werry, warye, mare, mere*, seven MSS, Hg Bo[2]

[1] M–R, iii, 441.   [2] M–R, iii, 142.   [3] See Robinson's note, p. 685.
[4] Jordan, *Handbuch der Mittelenglischen Grammatik* (2nd ed.: Heidelberg, 1934),
§ 163.

El Ad[3] Hk Lc Mg, which represent at least four independent lines of transmission, give the form that has been read as *uerye*.[1] The initial letter is interesting: normally, of course, initial *u* and *v* are both represented scribally by *v*, and the two-minim initial ordinarily represents *n*, not *u*. On the face of it, one would expect the combination of two minims plus *-erye* to give *nerye*, and I wonder whether that was not what O[1] really did intend.[2] *Nerian*, 'to save', is, of course, common in OE in theological associations: compare *Ner(i)gend*, 'the Saviour'.[3] The *OED* does not, however, list the verb, which apparently went out of currency with the Conquest. Nevertheless, it might well have been preserved in charms such as the carpenter's, which has all the earmarks of being an ancient one, or at least a recollection of an ancient one. Observe particularly *Benedight*, representing the normal development of the Latin *Benedictus* which was used by OE writers, generally displaced in ME by the French forms *Beneit*, *Benet*. And, as is well-known, the personified Pater Noster plays a part in the OE *Solomon and Saturn*.[4]

If one may read an initial *n*, then the line—which in any case seems to require a verb—means, 'May the White Pater Noster save (us) from (the perils of the) night'. I take *nerye* to be the third person singular of the present subjunctive, a form in which the *i*-suffix of verbs of the first weak OE class would normally be preserved into ME of the South and West.[5] Since the OE verb is transitive, the lack of an expressed object is difficult if one assumes that Chaucer knew exactly what John was saying, but the object may be taken to be implicit in the *hous* (in turn implying its inhabitants) of the preceding line; or alternatively, if Chaucer remembered the charm phonetically rather than by its sense, *nyghtes* might be taken as reflecting an original *night us*. As it stands, *nyghtes* seems to be a generalized plural meaning

---

[1] All MSS-readings are from M-R, iii, 142, and v, 346.

[2] The forms *mare*, *mere*, if not merely wild glosses, also suggest a misreading of a two-minim initial.

[3] See Bosworth-Toller under words cited.

[4] Ed. R. J. Menner (New York, 1941).

[5] Samuel Moore, *Historical Outlines of English Sounds and Inflections*, rev. by A. H. Marckwardt (Ann Arbor, 1951), pp. 119, 122, 124, says that in the South the *i*-suffix was preserved through the 13th century and in Kent even later, but in the West was displaced before the end of the 12th; but the B-text MSS of *Piers Plowman* show preservation well into the 15th century in certain areas of the South and West.

'night-time', or nights collectively;[1] it is governed by the preposition *for* meaning 'as a precaution against'[2]—or, as we should say, and some of the scribes did say,[3] 'from the night'. ME idiom would, in this context, require the El reading *For nyghtes*, preferred by Robinson, Koch, Skeat, and the *Globe*, rather than Hg *For the nyghtes*, preferred by Manly and Rickert. It is possible that the definite article was introduced by scribes who assumed that *nyghtes* was a genitive modifying a following noun.

The corrected reading by no means clears up all the problems the charm presents.[4] Nor is it itself entirely certain. But it seems better to prefer a reading that conforms with scribal practice and that has some etymological respectability to even more uncertain *verye* or *uerye*—perhaps ghosts of a sort never imagined by carpenter John.

[1] See *OED*, *nights*.
[2] See *OED*, *for*, prep., 23, d.
[3] For the preposition, Cn En[1] Fi Ha[4](2) Ld[1] Py read *fro*; Tc[2] *from*; the rest *for*. The definite article is omitted by Cx[1] Dl El Ha[4] He Ii Ne Tc[2] To. Uninflected *nyght* is given by Bo[1] Cn Fi La Lc Ma Mg Ph[2] Ra[1].
[4] I suspect that in the last line the pronoun *thow* should be repeated before *seinte* as in many *MSS*.

10

PATRISTIC EXEGESIS IN THE CRITICISM OF MEDIEVAL LITERATURE: THE OPPOSITION

I AM NOT AWARE of any valid theoretical objection to the use of patristic exegesis in the criticism of medieval literature: if, as D. W. Robertson, Jr, says,[1] it is true that all serious poetry written by Christians during the Middle Ages promotes the doctrine of charity by using the same allegorical structure that the Fathers found in the Bible, then it follows that patristic exegesis alone will reveal the meaning of medieval poetry, and it would be sheer folly to disapprove of the fact. And even if one disbelieves, as I do, that the generality of good medieval poetry is such single-minded allegory, it would still be foolish to ignore the influence of the patristic tradition on medieval poetry, including that of the great poets Chaucer and Langland. But to admit such influence is not at all the same thing as admitting either that poetry which is nonallegorical in manner must be allegorical in meaning or that allegorical poetry which does not seem to be promoting charity must in fact be promoting it. There may be a handful of such poems, but I doubt that they are very good, or, if they are good, that they are good because they are cryptically allegorical or charity-promoting. In any case, I know of no such poems in Middle English, which is the only field in which I am competent. The patristic influence on Middle English poetry seems

---

[1] 'Historical Criticism', in *English Institute Essays 1950*, ed. A. S. Downer (New York, 1951), p. 14.

to me to consist in providing occasional symbols which by their rich tradition enhance the poetic contexts they appear in, but which are called into use naturally by those contexts and are given fresh meaning by them.

It is scarcely necessary to reassert the right of a poem to say what it means and mean what it says, and not what any one, before or after its composition, thinks it ought to say or mean. The existence of this right gives me, I hope, the right to test the validity of a kind of criticism which, it seems to me, imposes a categorical imperative upon the critic to operate in a certain way regardless of how the poem is telling him to operate. Since I lack a theoretical objection to patristic criticism as such, I can justify my opposition to it only by the invidious method of analyzing specific patristic critiques; but surely the burden of the proof is on the proponents of the critical method, who deny that I can understand what I read without possessing their special knowledge. To excuse my invidiousness I shall invoke a passage from the Scriptures: By their fruits ye shall know them. This I shall apply with twofold reference—though not, I trust, allegorically: that is, I shall apply it not only to those who try to prove the necessity for patristic exegesis, but also to the works in which this necessity is supposed to exist. I shall try to suggest that to give a reader a flat injunction to find one predetermined specific meaning in Middle English poetry is anything but the ideal way of preparing him to understand something old and difficult and complicated; for in his eagerness to find what must be there he will very likely miss what is there; and in so doing he may miss a meaning arising from the poem that is better than anything that exegesis is able to impose upon it. I hope I shall not offend any one if I suggest that while charity is the most important of doctrines it is not the only subject worth writing about, and that many poems may conduce to charity without mentioning it either specifically or allegorically. I may say rather ruefully that one of the natural disadvantages of the opponent of patristic criticism is that he is constantly being put in the position of seeming to deny that the Fall of Man has any dominant importance in the history of man's thought just because he denies that it has any relevance in a specific literary work. There are, indeed, moments when I could wish that scholars in Middle

English literature would remind themselves that they are not angels but anglicists.

Having gone so far, I might go on to suggest that the Fathers of the Church were less expert at devising rules for poets than they were at devising rules for Christians. I am not, however, entirely persuaded that they did devise rules for poets. The case for the generalization that medieval poets were enjoined by patristic authority to write nothing but allegories supporting charity seems rather less than crystal-clear. It was natural that the fourfold method of scriptural interpretation should exert an influence on secular poets, especially in view of its occasional extension to the great pagan poets; and of course some medieval poets were, like Dante, deeply interested in exalting Christian doctrine through their poetry and consciously used allegory—even, perhaps, four-level allegory—to do so. But this does not mean that they all felt obliged to behave like Dante. I may quite well be wrong, but I cannot find that any of the patristic authorities ever clearly exhorted secular poets to write as the Bible had been written, even though the inference is pretty strong that some of them would have so exhorted if they had got round to it. But it seems to me that in order to find a definite injunction the modern critic has consciously to make a large inference.[1] Nor do I think that the case is much supported by the fact that in medieval schools reading was taught with attention to three matters, the *littera* or text, the *sensus* or narrative statement, and the *sententia* or theme, since the identification of *sententia* with an allegory promoting charity is itself no more than an inference.[2] After all, competent poetry has always contained something more than words making a statement, something that might well be called *sententia*, and I should imagine that Greeks, Romans, Arabs, Jews, and other non-Christians might inevitably teach poetry according to the same system: does the *Iliad* have

---

[1] See the historical treatment of the matter by Robertson in the essay cited above and in 'Some Medieval Literary Terminology, with Special Reference to Chrétien de Troyes', *SP*, xlviii (1951), 669–92; also the treatment by Robertson and B. F. Huppé in the first chapter of *Piers Plowman and Scriptural Tradition* (Princeton, 1951). The evidence for a genuine claim by Dante that he was using fourfold allegory in the *Divine Comedy* seems weakened by such recent studies as R. H. Green's 'Dante's "Allegory of Poets" and the Mediaeval Theory of Poetic Fiction', *Comparative Literature*, ix (1957), 118–28.

[2] See Roberton, 'Historical Criticism', p. 13, and Huppé and Robertson, p. 1.

no *sententia* because it is not Christian? Finally, there is at least one dissenting vote in the roll call of theologians presumably enjoining poets to write allegory after the example of Scripture. As W. K. Wimsatt pointed out in a paper on this topic several years ago,[1] Thomas Aquinas makes the unequivocal statement that 'in no intellectual activity of the human mind can there properly speaking be found anything but literal sense: only in Scripture, of which the Holy Ghost was the author, man the instrument, can there be found' the spiritual sense—that is, the four levels of allegory.[2] While I recognize that St Thomas is not a Father and that his statement may be idiosyncratic (as I believe some scholars regard it),[3] nevertheless I think he ought to be honestly reckoned with. To date I have seen no real discussion of his opinion by supporters of patristic exegesis. Nor will I accept as reputable the excuse that because he was a friar St Thomas would hardly reflect the point of view of such medieval poets as favoured the monks.[4]

I shall support my opposition to patristic exegesis in its extreme and most common form by examining three examples from its literature: critiques of *Piers Plowman*, of a poem by Chaucer, and of a Middle English lyric. I have naturally chosen the examples that seem to serve my purposes best, but this partiality is somewhat compensated for by the fact that these analyses have been taken as models by those who practise patristic exegesis. To the reasonable question of whether there are in existence specimens of patristic exegesis which do not arouse my opposition, I give a qualified yes; these concern poems where the Christian preoccupation is clearly a marked feature of the poem and where this sort of exegesis may help to enrich our appreciation of the poet's handiwork. My opposition begins, however,

---

[1] Wimsatt, 'Two Meanings of Symbolism: A Grammatical Exercise', *Catholic Renascence*, viii (1955), 19: I am indebted to Mr Wimsatt's excellent paper for this reference to St Thomas.

[2] *Quaestiones Quodlibetales*, vii, Quaestio vi, Art. xvi: Unde in nulla scientia, humana industria inventa, proprie loquendo, potest inveniri nisi litteralis sensus; sed solum in ista Scriptura, cujus Spiritus sanctus est auctor, homo vero instrumentum.

[3] Green ('Dante's "Allegory of Poets"', p. 121) speaks of St Thomas's *effort* 'to restrict the term *allegoria* to the mode of Sacred Scripture'.

[4] Huppé and Robertson (p. 10) say that they in general exclude the commentaries of friars because Langland was anti-fraternal.

when the author of the critique tries to substitute a special meaning for the one the poem yields without exegesis, an attempt that is common enough to seem characteristic of the current school of exegetes.[1]

Christian preoccupation is certainly a marked feature of *Piers Plowman*, and on the surface of it the poem appears admirably suited to patristic exegesis. It is, in the first place, an allegory that promotes charity (though sometimes in a rather malevolent way); its author frequently cites the Fathers of the Church; it uses symbols, such as the Tree of Charity and Patience, that come from the patristic tradition; its meaning is occasionally so murky that one must invoke every sort of aid to understanding (not, I think, one of the poem's virtues); and, most important, it not only is based in large part upon biblical texts, but it frequently quotes the Scriptures, so that we should expect patristic interpretations to show up along with the passages they interpret. Here, if anywhere, is favourable soil for the plow drawn by the four oxen who ornament the title page of Huppé and Robertson's book, *Piers Plowman and Scriptural Tradition*. I am therefore the more disappointed by what the book itself contains.

Every one will recall the opening of the B-Text. On a May morning the speaker goes to sleep among the Malvern Hills and dreams that he sees before him

> . . . a towr on a toft, trieliche ymaked,
> A deep dale binethe, a dungeon therinne
> With deepe diches and derke, and dredful of sighte.
> A fair feeld ful of folk foond I therbitweene
> Of al manere of men, the mene and the riche,
> Worching and wandring as the world asketh.
>
> (B-Prologue, ll.14–19)

The critics begin their analysis of the poem with the statement, 'In *Piers Plowman* the basic contrast between Jerusalem and Babylon is suggested at once by the dreamer's opening vision of the Tower of Truth, the Dungeon of Hell, and, in between, the

---

[1] R. P. Miller, in 'Chaucer's Pardoner, the Scriptural Eunuch, and the Pardoner's Tale', *Speculum*, xxx (1955), 180–99, for instance, gives an excellent account of the patristic significance of the Pardoner's condition; but when he replaces Chaucer's spiritual (and physical) eunuch with the Fathers' scriptural eunuch, he seems to me to be depreciating the poem.

Field of Folk'.[1] This is certainly true, but nevertheless the phrasing of the statement causes me discomfort. Some one who had not read the poem carefully, or who had read only part of it, might very well get the idea that Langland habitually deals in terms of the compound patristic symbol Jerusalem vs. Babylon: the critics' phrasing surely suggests his easy familiarity with the patristic tradition. Yet the symbol here is the critics' and not Langland's. Indeed, while in his poem Jerusalem appears again and again with all its ancient symbolism upon it, Babylon is never hell, but just a foreign city. Instead of employing the patristic allegory of the two cities, the poet is content to give us two towers, one on a hillock, one in a dale, one fair, one ugly, but in any case towers of the kind that dotted the medieval English landscape. Since the critics fail to derive the towers from patristic sources, one might suggest that the poet had eschewed tradition for everyday reality, as poets often do: his own practical sensibility saw the great contrast as between the soaring watchtower (Watchman, tell us of the night) and the sullen keep (which is the night). And if this is going too far, one can at least, I think, say that the critics are guilty of smuggling in patristic symbolism at the very outset of their journey.

Let us proceed to their following sentences: 'It is significant that the Folk are not assembled in an orderly pilgrimage toward the Tower [i.e., of Truth]: they are occupied with the world. . . . This situation represents the underlying problem in the poem. The folk of the world are preoccupied with worldly affairs, "wandryng" in confusion.'[2] Now this, I submit, is unwarranted intrusion upon the poem. It has not said or even hinted that the folk of the field are wrong in being occupied with the world; 'worching and wandring' suggests that some of them are occupied with the world in the right way, some in the wrong way; but in either case, being in the world, they are necessarily concerned with it. The disapproval of this fact is not the poet's, but the critics'. St Augustine might, in one of his more world-hating moments, have agreed with them, but he was not writing *Piers Plowman*. And indeed the critics suggest by their next sentence that in pursuing Augustine they have perhaps tripped on Langland. 'But not all of them [the Folk] seem hopeless. The dreamer's attention is at once called to the hard working plowmen.'[1]

> Some putten hem to the plow, played ful selde,
> In setting and in sowing swonken ful harde,
> And wonnen that wastours with glutonye destroyeth.

(B-Prologue, ll.20–2)

Now if I rightly understand the purport of the critics' remarks, these hard-working plowmen ought to be off on an orderly pilgrimage to the Tower of Truth, which, I take it, would make them somewhat better than merely not hopeless. And, of course, the image of life as a pilgrimage to Truth, or the Celestial City, is a time-honoured one:

> This world nis but a thurghfare ful of wo,
> And we been pilgrimes passing to and fro.

Furthermore it is an image which Langland does, at times, invoke, but not here. For the poem is not considering just now the good man's life allegorically as a pilgrimage to Truth but literally as a life of productive work. The poem does indeed concern salvation, but it also recognizes the practical fact that salvation in the next world depends upon one's actions in this, and while it points the way to heaven it is also concerned with tidying up earth. The pilgrimage of the hard-working plowmen is their hard work. Later on in the poem Piers Plowman himself, like Huppé and Robertson, momentarily identifies the allegorical with the literal when he volunteers to leave off plowing and lead a pilgrimage to Truth; but Truth tells him in no uncertain terms to stay home and keep on plowing.[2] It is appropriate to notice here what St Thomas repeats from St Augustine about the fourfold interpretation of Scripture: 'There is nothing darkly related in any part of Holy Writ which is not clearly revealed elsewhere'.[3] In this case the critics have detected a dark pronouncement on the management of earthly affairs which the poem clearly controverts later. Plowmen by definition ought to plow.

Huppé and Robertson continue: 'Unfortunately, the plowmen

---

[1] Ibid.   [2] See especially B-Text vii.1–5.

[3] *Quodlibetales*, vii, Quaestio vi, Art. xiv: nihil est quod occulte in aliquo loco sacrae Scripturae tradatur quod non alibi manifeste exponatur.

are accompanied by false plowmen, by persons who dress as plowmen through pride':[1]

> And some putten hem to pride, apparailed hem therafter,
> In countenance of clothing comen disgised. (B-Prologue, ll.23–4)

While these lines directly follow the description of the plowmen, the only way one can turn the proud men they mention into false plowmen is by taking as the antecedent of the adverb *therafter* not the noun *pride*, which immediately precedes it, but the plowmen of three lines before. Now one may reasonably doubt that any one at all in the Middle Ages would, through pride, dress as a plowman, the lowest of the low; but this is as nothing to my doubt about the syntax which yields such an interpretation. It ought to be stated loudly that Middle English syntax, while it is different from that of Modern English and often far more colloquial, is wholly logical and bound by its own firm rules: it is not mere illiterate imprecision that permits one to read without regard for the niceties of correlation. Here the chances are about ninety-eight out of a hundred that *therafter* refers to pride; about one out of a hundred that it refers to *wastours*, which is the next closest antecedent; and about one out of a thousand that it refers to the plowmen. And certainly the natural sense is the best one: people filled with pride of worldly position dress up in fancy clothes. There are no false plowmen in the text: there are merely ornamental parasites contrasted with hard-working peasants.

The trouble is that the critics have been kidnapped by their preconceptions. Since they believe one of the most important themes of *Piers Plowman* to be that 'the function of those in the *status praelatorum* has been usurped by certain members of the *status religiosorum*'[2]—the friars have taken over the duties of the secular clergy—they are anxious to have the poet develop this theme at once. For, as it now appears, the poem's plowmen are not just 'simple peasants',[3] but represent, in the patristic tradition, 'the true followers of the prelatical life'.[4] Naturally, if the true plowmen are the displaced prelates, the poem ought at once to have mentioned the false plowmen—the friars—who

[1] Huppé and Robertson, p. 17.   [2] Ibid., p. 7.
[3] Ibid., p. 17.   [4] Ibid., p. 19.

have displaced them. We have seen how the text is made to do what it ought to have done. But the simple literal reading does not permit false plowmen. Furthermore, I am sure that the plowmen of the Prologue represent not prelates, but plowmen, men who are doing a necessary part of the dirty work exacted by this world. Having spent a good deal of time with the poem, I am aware that a plowman may be an image for a spiritual plowman, which is what Piers Plowman is or becomes in the course of the poem; but I hope that the first time I read the poem I had enough sensitivity to it to realize that the word *plowmen* was loaded, even without benefit of the Fathers. On the other hand, I do not think that I said at this point, 'Hah, "plowmen", *id est, praelati*'. Nor do I think that any contemporary reader would have, though he might well have thought of all hard-working honest men, including priests. If he had said that, one cannot help wondering what he would have said when, a little later in the same catalogue of folk, he encounters parish priests. What in the world (or out of it) do they represent?

I shall pass over the remainder of Huppé and Robertson's interpretation of the catalogue of folk, merely pausing to observe that it seems wantonly to confuse the literal and the metaphorical. There are anchorites who are said to represent anchorites, merchants who are said to represent the whole laity, minstrels who are said to represent 'those who use the goods of the world properly for the worship of God, who praise the Lord without desire for temporal reward'[1]—despite the fact that they 'get gold with their glee' (B-Prologue, l.34), japers and janglers who are said to represent 'those who profess the faith but do not work accordingly'; and finally beggars who are allowed to represent beggars, pardoners pardoners, priests priests, and bishops bishops. Any cryptographer who keeps forgetting his code and writing plain English is simply incompetent; I do not think Langland was incompetent or, for that matter, a cryptographer.

I shall conclude this part of my paper with one final analysis. Shortly after his vision of the Field of Folk the dreamer sees a vision of the founding of an earthly kingdom:

[1] Ibid., p. 22.

Thanne cam ther a king, knighthood him ladde,
Might of the comunes made him to regne;
And thanne cam Kinde Wit, and clerkes he made,
For to conseille the king and the comune save.
The king and knighthood and clergye bothe
Casten that the comune sholde [hir comunes] finde.
The comune contreved of Kinde Wit craftes,
And for profit of alle the peple plowmen ordaigned,
To tilie and to travaile as trewe lif asketh.
The king and the comune and Kinde Wit the thridde
Shoop lawe and lewtee, eech [lif] to knowe his owne.[1]

(B-Prologue ll.112–22)

I had always thought this an idealized picture of the political community. A king, supported by his knights and by the common people, counselled by clerks, assisted at every turn by Natural Intelligence, in order to serve the common profit and to fulfill the demands of a life of integrity, creates law and justice and assigns each component of the kingdom its place, so that every man should know his privileges and responsibilities. Apparently I was wrong, for the king's council

did not consist of a representative body of his subjects; it was made up of clerks appointed by Kind Wit or *scientia*. The king, his barons, and the clergy, neglecting their responsibilities, decided that the commons must take care of themselves, so that the commons, also resorting to *scientia*, found it necessary to establish 'plowmen'. Together, the king and his commons, guided by *scientia*, formulated law and loyalty for the protection of private property, 'eche man to knowe his owne'.[2]

My errors had been many. I had not realized that representative government was a patristic ideal: I had thought it the ideal of a rather anti-patristic rationalism. I had not known that Kinde Wit was *scientia* and a villainously unreliable faculty: I had rather supposed the poet approved of it, since he very frequently couples it with Conscience; and Dunning and Hort exalt it almost to the position of modern 'conscience' and 'reason'.[3] I had

[1] The emendations seem obvious, though, as the following quotation from Huppé and Robertson shows, Skeat's text reads *man* for *lif* and *hemself* for *hir comunes*: the reference of either pronoun—*hemself* or *hir*—is ambiguous.

[2] Huppé and Robertson, p. 27.

[3] T. P. Dunning, *Piers Plowman: An Interpretation of the A-Text* (Dublin, 1937), pp. 39 ff; Greta Hort, *Piers Plowman and Contemporary Religious Thought* (London, n.d.), pp. 69 ff.

not been aware that king, knights, and clergy were neglecting their responsibility for taking care of the commons: for it had not occurred to me that the defenders and adminstrators of the realm ought to be out producing food, which is what I thought the verb *finden* meant and which I had assumed was a function of the commons, and specifically of plowmen. Nor had it become clear to me that the creation of law was a conspiracy to protect private property: I had thought that law and justice—which is what *lewtee* seems to mean—made possible social order, and that social order was desirable in this miserable world.

But my worst mistake was in connection with the last phrase of the passage, 'each man [*lif*] to know his own', which I had once written was 'the most significant phrase for understanding [the poet's] idea of earthly government'.[1] I should have said 'misunderstanding'. For the two critics write of it: 'That this is not a proper goal is evident from I Cor. 10.24: *Nemo quod suum est quaerat*'.[2] Let no man seek his own. They go on, quite correctly, to define the seeking of one's own as cupidity, the opposite of charity, and hence the negative side of the principle which, according to them, is the theme of all medieval literature.

You may remember that at the end of the Rat Parliament in the B-Prologue a little mouse taunts the rats with their failure to bell the cat and offers the cold consolation that it was a bad idea in the first place. The mouse ends his speech with the line,

Forthy eech a wis wight I warne, wite wel his owene.

Therefore I warn each wise wight to wit well his own. Needless to say, under the scrutiny of the critics this turns out to be a very wicked little rodent indeed, counselling the rats, like Belial, to slothful ease, or, like Mammon, to seeking wealth and heeding not St Paul's injunction. But the truth is that he is no more telling the rats to seek their own than law is encouraging men to seek their own in the earlier passage. I once wrote that 'without risk of error, one may add the word *place* or *part* in order to make the phrase meet the requirements of modern idiom: each man, and therefore each class, should know and keep his own

[1] *Piers Plowman: The C-Text and Its Poet* (New Haven, 1949), pp. 109–10.
[2] Huppé and Robertson, p. 27.

place'.[1] Furthermore, I remain persuaded that this is what the phrase means, and that knowledge of one's own place in the world is a cardinal point in medieval theorizing of the most idealistic kind, that it is a principle upon which all order in this world depends: I'll bet it is in the Fathers. The truth is that Huppé and Robertson have on two occasions mistranslated Middle English to make a point that is not only entirely foreign to the poem's but directly opposed to it and disproved by other passages within the poem. They have made an ideal state a wicked one; and they have made of a poet counselling forbearance a revolutionary. In order to do this, they have taken first Middle English *knowen*, then *witen*, as the equivalents of Latin *quaerere*; they have made knowing the same as seeking. Once again it is relevant to quote St Thomas on scriptural interpretation: 'The spiritual sense is always based upon the literal sense, and proceeds from it'.[2] The literal sense of *to know* is 'to know'.

It seems to me that the failure which the two critics suffer with regard to the literal sense in the beginning of their analysis is repeated again and again as the analysis proceeds. It is patently unfair to condemn a whole work on the basis of a few pages, but I do not consider the sample uncharacteristic. The authors seem constantly to be contorting the text to find the message they want to find. This tendency reaches a kind of open confirmation in their discussion of the meaning of the protagonist's name, Will. After pointing out, I think rather suggestively, that Will, like the human will, 'moves between the opposites of willfulness and charity', they go on to observe: 'Because the poet has been successful as a poet, he has created in Will so appealingly human a character that through interest in him many have lost sight of the fact that Will is merely a device by means of which the poet may set off the actual against the ideal in the poem and so develop his major theme'.[3] It is fair to read this as saying that because the poet has been a good poet, he has been a poor teacher, and one might work out the proposition, the better the poet, the worse the teacher, and vice versa. Ultimately one has the

---

[1] Donaldson, *Piers Plowman: The C-Text*, p. 110.

[2] *Quodlibetales*, vii, Quaestio vi, Art. xiv: sed sensus spiritualis semper fundatur super litteralem, et procedit ex eo.

[3] Huppé and Robertson, p. 240.

poem going in one direction and its teaching going in the opposite. Under these circumstances I should prefer to follow the poem rather than outsiders who are telling me what it means to be saying.

There are, of course, good things in Huppé and Robertson's book. But curiously enough, these are in general not concerned with patristic exegesis, but are the insights of two excellent minds that have thought long and hard about the poem. The poet himself, when he is following patristic tradition, tends to explain his use of symbols in such a way that a reader ignorant of the tradition can understand them from the text—though of course knowledge of the tradition will enhance the reader's appreciation. Thus when the dreamer meets some one called Abraham representing faith, the first thing that Abraham says is, 'I am Faith' (BXVI.176). A character named Hope appears only to say at once that he has been given a 'maundement' upon the Mount of Sinai (BXVII.2). The most heavily patristic passage in the poem, that describing the Tree of Charity (BXVI.1–89), is also well-glossed by the poet—rather better glossed by him, I think, than by Huppé and Robertson. Scholars must, indeed, be grateful to the critics for the information they provide about the patristic background, a field in which they are enormously learned. But I can think of little that they say on the subject which the poem does not say equally well. And when, as in the passages I have analyzed, they substitute a remote allegory for the easy sense, they are letting their desire to show patristic influence override the simple demands of Middle English.

Having shown what I think to be a failure with regard to the *littera* of a medieval poem, let me turn to what I consider a failure with regard to the *sensus*. The Nun's Priest's Tale has always been one of Chaucer's most popular and at the same time most elusive works: one is apt to come away from this feast feeling that one has been abundantly fed, but one is not sure on what kind of food. No simple critical formula explains the reader's delight in the poem, which has so little plot and such enormous rhetorical dilation. Since the scholarly mind naturally abhors a vacuum of this sort, it is inevitable that a number of attempts should be made to show that the little plot is weighty enough to compensate for and even to overbalance the infinite expansiveness of the narrator. Of several attempts of this sort more or less concerned with the patristic tradition, I shall choose that of Mortimer Donovan, since his is the most specifically patristic.[1]

According to Donovan, the morality of the Nun's Priest's Tale —or sermon, as he prefers to call it—emerges only if one understands the patristic significance of the personages concerned. The poor widow who owns Chauntecleer and his several wives is the Church;[2] the fox is either the Devil or a heretic, or rather, both;[3] the rooster, originally a symbol of alertness,[4] comes, in the course of the analysis, to represent the alert Christian, though strictly speaking he should represent an alert priest; Dame Pertelote is, of course, woman, whose counsel Chauntecleer, through lechery, has listened to 'against his own superior judgment'.[5] The climax of the action in which these figures share is, according to the critic,

reached as Chauntecleer rides uncomfortably on the fox's back. Since Christian hope extends to the last, the once uxorious Chauntecleer now turns for divine aid against an adversary as powerful as Daun Russell, and, with all the alertness of his celebrated nature, he begs help. He knows with Chaucer's Parson that 'for as muchel as the devil fighteth agayns a man moore by queyntise and by sleighte than by strengthe, therfor men shal withstonden hym by wit and by resoun and by discrecioun.' ... So, begging divine help, he devises a plan which shows a return of reason.[6]

And so the alert Christian defeats the Devil-heretic in the nick of time.

There is no way of proving that the widow does not represent the Church—unless, of course, we apply to the tale St Augustine's and St Thomas's stricture that nothing is darkly said in one place that is not clearly revealed elsewhere. But I doubt that the fox represents the Devil or that Chauntecleer represents the alert Christian, not with seven wives. There were, if I may say so, foxes long before there were devils, and roosters were crowing off the hours long before Christians heard them. One might say that if there were no Devil a poultry-keeping farmer would

---

[1] 'The *Moralite* of the Nun's Priest's Sermon', *JEGP*, lii (1953), 498–508.
[2] Ibid., p. 505.   [3] Ibid., pp. 498 ff.   [4] Ibid., pp. 501 ff.
[5] Ibid., p. 506.   [6] Ibid., pp. 506–7.

have invented one in order to describe a fox, so that we hardly need Rabanus Maurus to explain the similarity between fox and devil, any more than we need Hugh of St Victor to tell us that the cock in his hourly crowing makes a good natural example of attention to duty.[1] What we have here in poetic (or barnyard) terms is a devilish fox-villain and a conscientious, if foolish, rooster-hero. I am willing to accept the premise that Pertelote represents woman, though I think it's unkind of the critic to repeat the Nun's Priest's slander that Chauntecleer took her advice, something the Nun's Priest suggests in his eagerness to blame Chauntecleer's misfortune on anything and everything except Chauntecleer. Actually, Pertelote had advised certain medicines, but Chauntecleer had defied them, heroically, just as he defied dreams: Adam Rooster was at least able to resist eating Eve Hen's hellebore, and thereby maintained a kind of integrity, if a prideful and lecherous one.

On first reading Donovan's criticism I thought he had inadvertently left out Chauntecleer's prayer for divine aid—which I couldn't recall—for all he quotes is Chauntecleer's speech to the fox:

> ... Sire, if that I were as ye,
> Yit sholde I sayn, *as wis God helpe me*,
> 'Turneth again, ye proude cherles alle!
> A verray pestilence upon you falle!'

Then I realized that the words 'as wis God helpe me', as surely as God help me, were italicized,[2] and were, indeed, the prayer that Chauntecleer uttered 'with all the alertness of his celebrated nature'. But even this crumb is not really available: the prayer qualifies the apodasis of a contrary-to-fact condition, in a position safely removed from the actual Chauntecleer; and it is, indeed, not a prayer at all, but an oath of which Chaucer's Parson would not have approved.

Even if one were to accept the allegorical interpretation of this tale I cannot see that much has, critically speaking, been gained. If one connects things up with a specific Christian doctrine one does, to be sure, introduce a kind of weightiness into the discussion, but in this case it seems a deadweight of which the poem

| [1] Ibid., p. 501.   [2] Ibid., p. 507.

were better relieved. I must say, in all seriousness, that if the *sentia* of the Nun's Priest's Tale, the quality which justifies our reading the tale, is that the alert Christian with God's help can thwart the Devil-heretic, then Chaucer has let us down with a thud. But I do not think he has. At the end of his critique, Donovan tells us that 'the identity of the cock and fox is almost lost behind what Professor Kittredge calls this "preacher's illustrative anecdote, enormously developed until it swallows up the sermon"'.[1] This seems a little like running out into the streets shouting 'Eureka!' only to discover that one has neglected to dress; for the fact is that the little anecdote on which the exegesis depends is only one tiny grain of wheat in an intolerable deal of chaff, and if it contains Chaucer's main point then he is guilty of the most horrid misproportioning. But one ought to trust the statistics of great poetry rather than those of critics, and any interpretation of a poem that ignores the bulk of it is likely to be wrong: a medieval teacher would have warned us to heed the *sensus* before extracting the *sententia*.

The Nun's Priest's Tale does have a real point, a serious point, and a better point than the one I reject, and it lies where one should expect to find it, in the enormous rhetorical elaboration of the telling. For rhetoric here is regarded as the inadequate defence that mankind erects against an inscrutable reality; rhetoric enables man at best to regard himself as a being of heroic proportions—like Achilles, or like Chauntecleer—and at worst to maintain the last sad vestiges of his dignity (as a rooster Chauntecleer is carried in the fox's mouth, but as a hero he rides on his back); rhetoric enables man to find significance both in his desires and in his fate, and to pretend to himself that the universe takes him seriously. And rhetoric has a habit, too, of collapsing in the presence of simple common sense. Chauntecleer is not an alert Christian; he is mankind trying to adjust the universe to his own specifications and failing—though not, I am happy to say, fatally. Donovan assumes that Chauntecleer has been cured of his uxoriousness—perhaps he is going to retire into voluntary widowhood. I am less sanguine. I fear he is going to go on behaving as the roosters and men of Western civilization have always behaved, preserving their dignity by artificial

[1] Ibid., p. 508.

11—S.O.C.

respiration and somewhat against the odds. In short, the fruit of the Nun's Priest's Tale is its chaff.[1]

I shall conclude with one final analysis of patristic exegesis, Robertson's interpretation of the little lyric 'Maiden in the Moor'.[2] In this poem we have the barest of literal statements and almost no *sensus* at all; one must proceed directly from the letter to the *sententia*. The poem is short; therefore I quote it entire:

> Maiden in the moor lay,
>   In the moor lay,
> Sevenight ful, sevenight ful;
> Maiden in the moor lay,
>   In the moor lay,
> Sevenightes ful and a day.
>
> Wel [i.e., good] was hir mete.
>   What was hir mete?
> The primerole and the—
> The primerole and the—
> Wel was hir mete.
>   What was hir mete?
> The primerole and the violet.
>
> Wel was hir dring.
>   What was hir dring?
> The chelde water of the—
> The chelde water of the—
> Wel was hir dring.
>   What was hir dring?
> The chelde water of the welle-spring.
>
> Wel was hir bowr.
>   What was hir bowr?
> The rede rose and the—
> The rede rose and the—
> Wel was hir bowr.
>   What was hir bowr?
> The rede rose and the lilye flowr.[3]

---

[1] For a fuller expression of this interpretation, see my *Chaucer's Poetry*, pp. 940–4.

[2] 'Historical Criticism', pp. 26–7.

[3] For the poem in its original form, see *Secular Lyrics of the XIVth and XVth Centuries*, ed. by R. H. Robbins (Oxford, 1947), pp. 12–13.

Of this charming little piece Robertson writes:

On the surface, although the poem is attractive, it cannot be said to make much sense. Why should a maiden lie on a moor for seven nights and a day? And if she did, why should she eat primroses and violets? Or again, how does it happen that she has a bower of lilies and roses on the moor? The poem makes perfectly good sense, however, if we take note of the figures and signs in it. The number seven indicates life on earth, but life in this instance went on at night, or before the Light of the World dawned. The day is this light, or Christ, who said, 'I am the day'. And it appears appropriately after seven nights, or, as it were, on the count of eight, for eight is also a figure of Christ. The moor is the wilderness of the world under the Old Law before Christ came. The primrose is not a Scriptural sign, but a figure of fleshly beauty. We are told three times that the primrose was the food of this maiden, and only after this suspense are we also told that she ate or embodied the violet, which is a Scriptural sign of humility. The maiden drank the cool water of God's grace, and her bower consisted of the roses of martyrdom or charity and the lilies of purity with which late medieval and early Renaissance artists sometimes adorned pictures of the Blessed Virgin Mary, and, indeed, she is the Maiden in the Moor. . . . [1]

I cannot find that the poem, as a poem, makes any more 'sense' after exegesis than it did before, and I think it makes rather more sense as it stands than the critic allows it. Maidens in poetry often receive curiously privileged treatment from nature, and readers seem to find the situation agreeable. From the frequency with which it has been reprinted it seems that the 'Maiden in the Moor' must have offered many readers a genuine poetic experience even though they were without benefit of the scriptural exegesis. I do not think that most of them would find it necessary to ask the questions of the poem that Robertson has asked; indeed, it seems no more legitimate to inquire what the maiden was doing in the moor than it would be to ask Wordsworth's Lucy why she did not remove to a more populous environment where she might experience a greater measure of praise and love. In each case the poetic *donnée* is the highly primitive one which exposes an innocent woman to the vast, potentially hostile, presumably impersonal forces of nature; and the Middle English lyric suggests the mystery by which these

---

[1] 'Historical Criticism', p. 27.

forces are, at times, transmuted into something more humane, even benevolent, by their guardianship of the innocent maiden. The poetic sense is not such as necessarily to preclude allegory, and I shouldn't be surprised if medieval readers often thought of the Virgin as they read the poem, not because they knew the symbols and signs, but because the Virgin is the paramount innocent maiden of the Christian tradition: such suggestivity is one of poetry's principal functions. Robertson's hard-and-fast, this-sense-or-no-sense allegory, however, seems to me so well-concealed and, when explicated, so unrevealing that it can be considered only disappointing if not entirely irrelevant. The function of allegory that is worth the literary critic's attention (as opposed to cryptography, which is not) cannot be to conceal, but is to reveal, and I simply do not believe that medieval poets veiled their poems in order to hide their pious message from heretics and unbelievers. In allegory the equation is not merely *a* equals *b*, the literal statement reanalyzed equals the suggested meaning, but is something more like *a* plus *b* equals *c*, the literal statement plus the meaning it suggests yield an ultimate meaning that is an inextricable union of both. Patristically the primrose may be a figure of fleshly beauty, but actually (and the actual is what poetry is made of) it is one of the commonest of the lovely flowers which nature in its benevolent aspect lavishes upon mankind and, in this case, all-benevolent lavishes upon the maiden of the moor. Robertson asks the question 'Why should she eat primroses?' I hope that if I answer 'Because she was hungry', it will not be said of me that a primrose by the river's brim a yellow primrose was to him, and it was nothing more.

I said at the beginning of this paper that I did not know of any valid theoretical objection to patristic criticism. I do, however, object to a procedure which substitutes for the art of the poet the learning or good intentions of the reader. Reading a poem intelligently is, I believe, one of the hardest things on earth to do:

Humankind cannot bear very much reality,

and I believe that great poetic art offers something very close to an ultimate reality. In order to read it well one has to put oneself into the impossible position of having all one's wits and faculties about one, ready to spring into activity at the first summons; yet, like hunting dogs, they must not spring before they are summoned; and only those that are summoned must spring; and the summons must come from the poem. To maintain oneself in this state of relaxed tension is frightfully fatiguing, and any serious reader will, I am sure, want to rest a good deal. This is fortunate for scholarship, since such activities as source study, investigation of historical context, philology, editing, and patristic exegesis are salubrious vacations from the awful business of facing a poem directly. For a good many people the interest implicit in such studies and the fun of them will become more important than the poems themselves, and this is understandable; and the activities I have mentioned and many more are as necessary and as honourable as literary criticism. I look forward myself to a year when the many incidental problems of editing *Piers Plowman* will, I hope, constantly distract me from the effort of understanding its meaning. But these activities are not the same as literary criticism, and none of them should be permitted to replace an interpretation of the poem arising from the poem. At certain periods source study, philology, historical orientation, and even some of the techniques of the new criticism have tended to obliterate the meaning of the poems with which they have associated themselves. It seems to me that patristic criticism is operating under a categorical imperative to do the same thing.

Robertson concludes his English Institute paper on patristic criticism with the remark that literature, 'regarded historically' —by which he means patristically—'can provide the food of wisdom as well as more transient aesthetic satisfactions'.[1] It is here that my disagreement with him becomes absolute. I do not feel that the effect that the poems of Chaucer and Langland and other poets have upon me is mere transient aesthetic satisfaction. I believe that a great work of art provides the reader with the food of wisdom because it is a great work of art. If this food is not specific Christian doctrine, I console myself that it emanates from a humane tradition that is as old as Western civilization and that Christianity has done much to preserve.

[1] Ibid., p. 31.

11

THE MYTH OF COURTLY LOVE

TO THIS YEAR (1965) in which we celebrate the seven hundred
and fiftieth anniversary of Magna Carta and the seven hundredth
anniversary of the birth of Dante, I should like to add another
significant event that medievalists ought to commemorate: the
eighty-second anniversary of *amour courtois*—or, as it is generally
mistranslated, courtly love. It is not, I suppose, strictly true that
courtly love had its Runnymede or Florence on page 519 of the
twelfth volume of *Romania*, for the equivalent of the phrase does
occur—apparently only once—in Provençal, in a poem by the
troubadour Pierre d'Auvergne. But it never seems to have
caught on until the end of the nineteenth century, when Gaston
Paris used the French term in a study of Chrétien de Troyes's
Chevalier de la Charrette, an essay which contained, inevitably,
side glances at Marie de Champagne, Andreas Capellanus,
Eleanor of Aquitaine, and the troubadours. For what it is worth,
I note that Paris placed the adjective *courtois* in italics, probably
in order to suggest the relationship with Provençal *cortezia*: I am
sorry that the practice was not carried over into English, for
'*courtly* love' has a sober, confining sound beside which the
normal English accentuation 'courtly *love*' seems positively in-
toxicating—a fact that may have influenced for the worse the
subsequent history of the subject.

In the eighty-odd years since the publication of Paris's article,
amour courtois has proved an extraordinarily fertile dragon's
tooth. Such well-documented concepts of antiquity as Greek
hybris, Latin *pietas*, Old English *wyrd*, and French *chevalerie* have
been the subject of much printed discussion by scholars-at-arms;
but I believe that the literature discussing courtly love out-
weighs the lot, and I had no idea, when I undertook this paper, of
how much writing on the topic I was not going to be able to

read. The idea of courtly love evidently appeals to two basic human desires: to find in the past something strikingly and excitingly different from the drab present, and to talk about love, especially a love that is suspected of being naughty, but whose naughtiness has attained archeological respectability. Indeed, courtly love provides so attractive a setting from which to study an age much preoccupied with love that if it had not existed scholars would have found it convenient to construct it—which, as a matter of fact, they have, at least partially, done. For apart from the single appearance in Provençal, medieval writers do not speak of courtly love: they speak of *fin amour, amor honestus, cortezia*, or, in English, of love. But for scholarly purposes these terms are apparently either too precise or too all-embracing to describe what one believes, or would like to believe, was a widely held attitude toward love peculiar to the Middle Ages.

I suppose there is nothing intrinsically wrong in promoting a Provençal rarity into a term for a major medieval concept, though it is curious that, with the honourable exception of Father Denomy, scholars treating courtly love seem either to believe that *amour courtois* with its equivalents in other languages was a common medieval phrase, or else to be willing to use it without fear of anachronism, even though they acknowledge Gaston Paris's part in establishing its currency. The real trouble with the term, however, is that no two scholars ever seem to mean the same thing by it, and on several occasions lately when I have publicly expressed scepticism about courtly love, I have found myself passionately and simultaneously rebutted by scholars whose own definitions were so wildly divergent from one another as to be mutually exclusive. The result is that a student who has been taught a definition of courtly love before he approaches medieval love poetry finds himself constantly having to bend the definition in order to fit the poetry, or—worse —to bend the poetry in order to fit the definition. Thus if he has been told that adultery is a basic ingredient in courtly love, he will be discomfited, to say the least, to have to accept in place of adultery such substitutes as fornication, frustration, idealiza- tion, madness, matrimony, or death; or if he clings to his defini- tion through thick and thin, he will suspect every love lyric, no matter how innocent, of representing an assault by the poet on the chastity of another man's wife. The fact is that a definition of courtly love based on all the literature of the Middle Ages is too broad to be useful, while one derived from only selected primary documents fits well only those documents from which it has been derived.

It is this second fact that I am principally concerned with here, particularly as it affects the problem of immorality that is implicit or explicit in so many definitions of courtly love. I shall take as my principal example the definition that many students of English literature almost automatically receive. C. S. Lewis, on the second page of that brilliant and influential book *The Allegory of Love*, lists the characteristics of courtly love, with admirable clarity and emphatic capitalization, as 'Humility, Courtesy, Adultery, and the Religion of Love'. What a wonderful beginning! I know of no sentence that has cast a deeper spell on readers, or has drawn more students to the Middle Ages, or has befuddled them more. Lewis goes on to discuss Chrétien de Troyes and Andreas Capellanus (from whom, indeed, he derived the definition), and the expectant reader is not disappointed. But only Lewis's craft as a writer can make one fail to notice that in the remainder of a large book—from page 44 through page 366 —there is very little adultery: of the four essential characteristics of courtly love the most exciting seems to have been still-born. Even Chaucer's *Troilus*, which provides the climax for the medieval part of the book, concerns the love of a bachelor for a widow. And, as a number of scholars led by Gervase Mathew have pointed out, in Middle English literature up to Malory adultery is a very minor motif. Indeed, illicit love of all kinds is apt to get perfunctory treatment in medieval England, so that naughty couples in the continental vernaculars are sometimes made to dwindle into marriage by their English redactors. Notable adultery in Middle English is mostly in Chaucer, and it is mostly of the fabliau type: if its heroes fulfill Lewis's requirement of the pursuit of adultery, they are wholly deficient in Humility and the Religion of Love: as for Courtesy, their *hende wordes* are belied by their busy *handes*, as with Nicholas in the Miller's Tale. Indeed, Chaucer's most courtly lover (in Lewis's sense) is not Troilus, but Nicholas's rival Absolon, whose undoubted Humility, Courtesy, and Religion of Love condemn him to total failure in Adultery. It is not insignificant that a doctrine Lewis treats with a good deal of solemnity has greater relevance for Chaucer's comic heroes, for whom it provides a kind of ideal of misbehaviour, than it does for his serious lovers, to whom I shall return briefly later.

The trouble with making definitions of courtly love, especially definitions involving moral judgments, is not only that different documents yield divergent data but also that a single document or a single body of related documents yields divergent data to different scholars. On this matter my ignorance has forced me into making a controlled experiment: since my Provençal is wholly insufficient, I have had to try to discover what the troubadours considered courtly love to be by reading those scholars who have based definitions of courtly love on the troubadours. By doing this I have gained two significant general-izations (I think if I had read more the number would have been much larger): first, that the troubadours normally loved married ladies with whom they wished, above all, to consummate their love; second, that the troubadours' chief desire was to achieve a state of idealized frustration—one scholar, indeed, seems to suggest that they loved married ladies so that they would not have to spoil their love by consummating it. Thus torn between two wings of Provençal scholarship—Eleanor of Aquitaine and Bernard de Ventadour on the left wing, Dante and Beatrice just out of sight on the right—I conclude what I am sure scholars more interested in the poetry than in definition would tell me: that in some poems some troubadours give one impression, and in other poems other troubadours, or the same ones, give other impressions. They do, I take it, share one tendency: to sublimate their love. That is, to quote the *Oxford English Dic-tionary*, 'they act upon [it] so as to produce a refined product'; or they 'transmute [it] *into* something higher, nobler, more sublime or refined'; or they 'refine [it] away *into* something un-real or non-existent; . . . reduce [it] to unreality'. I believe these processes constitute the most important contribution of the Middle Ages to profane love. What happened after one of the processes had taken place in any individual poet—whether he got his lady or something else—is either unclear or various, and is in any case not really the business of literary criticism.

Yet the example of the troubadours illustrates the point that the moral aspects of one's definition of courtly love are apt to be profoundly influenced by what one believes the historical situation to have been. If one credits the old statement that Bernard actually loved and was loved by Eleanor of Aquitaine, then it is apparent that one will emphasize the potentially immoral elements in the poetry. But this is dangerous, for obviously tales about adultery between historical poets and historical women may have first derived from a wish-fulfilling reading of the poetry; yet having achieved the status of historical facts, such tales then support the theory that the love poets were really intent on committing adultery, and that great ladies were generally compliant. Within this vicious circle love becomes ever more vicious. Furthermore, in our lack of any very good information on the details of daily life in medieval courts, one swallow—like Eleanor—does seem to make a summer. Such a definition of courtly love as C. S. Lewis's seems to be the result of a confusion on his part of literary criticism with supposedly objective historical facts which he derived mainly from the earlier literature he was examining. Adultery is in his definition because he thought it an historical fact, not because it applies to the main body of the works he considers.

The real villain behind Lewis's definition, and the supreme confuser of literature and history, is that codifier of the *ars honeste amandi*, Andreas the Chaplain. His is a work that has generally been treated, by literary critics like Lewis, not as literature, but as history or sociology—and for excellent reasons. In the first place, it is utterly explicit: one book which reports endless dialogues between men and women, usually of different classes, in which the male argues why the female should love him and she argues why she shouldn't; a second book which contains general discussions of who should love whom and why and how, gives the thirty-one rules of a love splendidly immoral, and is, like the first, interspersed with tortuous love-decisions handed down by such eminent ladies as Marie de Champagne and her mother; and finally a third book, often called 'characteristically medieval', in which the author repudiates the entire content of the first two. The circumstantial nature of all this invites, if not commands, the reader to set it in an historical context, and the fact that the Countess of Champagne did have a chaplain named André seems to give us a right to see here a true picture of late twelfth-century French *mores*. Did not Marie, whom Andreas quotes as an authority on non-marital love, give to Chrétien both the *matière* and the *sen* of his adulterous *Knight of the Cart*? And may Andreas's work not be read as a gloss to this courtliest of courtly love poems, and vice versa? Therefore Marie was probably a patron of Andreas, who may have written at her pleasure; and Andreas must have known Chrétien, and probably Marie patronized some troubadours: she was, after all, her mother's daughter and her way of life may have been influenced by her.

All this is excellently *ben trovato*, not excluding the modern connotations of the name Champagne. Yet the historian who has looked mostly deeply into the records of the Court—J. F. Benton—is not inclined to accept this version of its life unquestioningly. He points out that Andreas refers to himself as a chaplain of the royal court, and not of Champagne; that there is little likelihood that Marie ever saw her mother after the latter had left the French king and court; and that from what little is known of Marie it is not probable that she had either the desire or the temperament to preside over a court of immoral love, or, if she did, that the Count her husband, while he lived, would have let her get away with it. Finally, Benton observes that the significance of Andreas's book, specific as it seems, is not so clear as to prevent some recent scholars from refusing to take it at face value.

Chief among these is Professor D. W. Robertson of Princeton, who has made a careful analysis of the logic (or illogic) of the first two books of Andreas, in which the doctrine of honest (i.e., immoral) love is set forth, and has come to the conclusion that Andreas is actually being ironical—that he means the direct opposite of what he seems to be saying. I do not agree with Robertson's oft-stated premise that any serious work written in the Middle Ages that does not overtly promote St Augustine's doctrine of charity will be found, on close examination, to be doing so allegorically or ironically, nor do I agree that Andreas can be made to read as a good disciple of St Augustine. Yet I agree with Robertson that Andreas is not to be understood as seriously promulgating immoral doctrine. My impression is, after a rereading of the Chaplain that could not help being more exhausting than exhaustive, that Andreas hoped he was being funny, and that Robertson is quite right to point out that one Drouart la Vache records that in 1290, when some one gave him a copy of Andreas, 'after he had read a little of it, he found the book so pleasing and he laughed so much over it' that he ended up by translating it into French. If one approaches the work with the solemnity of a Lewis, one must indeed wonder what in the world Drouart was laughing at.

I say I think Andreas meant to be funny: my sense of humour is insufficiently robust for me to agree with Robertson and Drouart that he succeeded. Nevertheless, it is easy to see in what ways he thought he was producing a *jeu d'esprit* by rewriting Ovid's *Art of Love* and *Remedies of Love* for his own time and in one of its characteristic genres. The dialogues of Andreas's first book are a series of debates that adhere closely to the rules of the *débat* genre: the speaker's sole object is to score points, and in doing so it does not matter that he shifts his ground shamelessly, confuses cause and effect, blatantly contradicts himself, even alters such wisps of perceptible personality as the author has given him. Andreas has merely adopted Ovid's theme of adulterous love and medievalized it by subjecting it to scholastic analysis and by infusing it with that spiritualization of the erotic that the troubadours show—not, let me hasten to say, that there is anything very spiritual about Andreas beyond the assumption that immoral love is morally improving. Where Ovid assumed that people loved in response to a carnal urge, Andreas pretends that it is a spiritual duty. Having lived in a society which liked to debate about love—a society which we still seem to be in—he had the essentially playful idea of seeing to what outrageous lengths he could push arguments in favour of immoral love— how crazy a tower he could erect by balancing and counter-balancing bricks without using one ounce of the mortar of common sense. His high point in outrage is the opinion, which he ascribes to Marie, that love cannot exist within marriage because marriage does not admit jealousy and love cannot exist without jealousy. The mind boggles at having to answer that.

Not only is Andreas's first book a series of debates, but also the

discussions of the second book partake of the debater's technique, by which both sides of all questions are carefully examined. And the first two books taken together with the third,
which repudiates their doctrine, form a larger debate. Both
Lewis and Robertson take the third book seriously, and Lewis
includes it in a splendid sentence describing medieval retractions: 'We hear the bell clang; and the children, suddenly hushed
and grave, and a little frightened, troop back to their master.'
Somehow I don't see Andreas, though he was rather more
childish than most, as a member of this troop. For his retraction
is just as outrageous in its own way as what it retracts. If it
stopped where it started, with the acknowledgement that God
hates and will condemn the lustful, one might accept it as
serious; but it goes on—and on, while most serious retractions
are short—into ever-increasing anticlimax, showing at length
what a nuisance love is to the comfortable life, and ending with
an extended antifeminist tirade in which Andreas strives to out-
Hieronymo St Jerome. Not only would this seem a curious
apology to set before God, but also a strange dish to set before
Marie de Champagne. But I doubt that it was meant to be set
before either one. My guess is that, like the English debate between the Owl and the Nightingale, it was designed for clerical
ears, for ecclesiasts, probably celibates who were in no great
danger of having their morals ruined by it, but who were in-
tellectually alert and might appreciate a scholastic joke on the
love-talking ladies of the laity. One may charitably hope that
they did appreciate it, but Andreas's resources in the way of wit
seem severely limited, and reading his tract is a penance I should
gladly avoid. No wonder it has been taken seriously as sociology:
the reader tends to feel that no imagination could have produced
so paltry a fiction: therefore it must be true. Yet the *Ars Honeste
Amandi* has, I think, about as much to do with erotic practices in
Champagne at the end of the twelfth century as the debate of
The Owl and the Nightingale has to do with ornithology.

Now I do not deny for a moment that adultery existed as an
historical fact in Champagne, and in Provençal, too, as it existed
in Homer's Greece, and Ovid's Rome, and still exists in modern
America; and it also exists in the poetry of Homer, Ovid, the
troubadours, Chrétien, and in modern fiction. Furthermore, I

suppose that adulterers adopt the style of love that is current in their culture, and that some medieval adulterers managed, like Lancelot, to feel that their adultery was sublime. But I do not believe that the proposition, which is insisted upon by Andreas, that love can exist only extra-maritally was ever much practised—that it ever had much counterpart in reality. It does not even seem to have much effect on the subsequent literature of supposedly courtly love: the Rose of Guillaume de Lorris's *Roman* can hardly be seen as a married woman; Marie de France's adulterous couples (who are relatively few in number) seem to fall in love naturally enough, not in response to a categorical imperative that wedlock must be broken; and so it is with Aurelius, the would-be adulterer in Chaucer's Breton Lay, the Franklin's Tale; and, as I have already indicated, Middle English literature exists in serene disregard of Andreas.

There seems to be a curious paradox in some definitions of courtly love: those scholars who place most emphasis on a supposed cult of adultery are often the very ones who, like Lewis, are most anxious to moralize the Middle Ages. I cannot explain this paradox, though I sometimes darkly suspect that a moral scholar who establishes within a highly moral medieval world a grossly immoral antibody hopes that he can thereby draw off some of the guilt from great writers who treat of illicit love when, morally speaking, they ought to have known better. That is, it was all right for writers to treat such subjects because a powerful tradition sanctioned it—provided, of course, that they trooped back to their master when the bell clanged. Thus F. N. Robinson, in emphasizing the importance of courtly love to an understanding of Chaucer's *Troilus*, says that 'It was expected that love should be sought outside of marriage'. Not only is this inaccurate, for Troilus and Criseide do not so much seek love as have it thrust upon them, but it also seems to reflect an oddly prim notion of people and of poets. Medieval secular writers, as opposed, perhaps, to many homilists, seem to me often to have been concerned more with what we should call spiritualization than with what we now call moralization: the troubadours suggest this, as does even Andreas in his flat-footed way. Chaucer's *Troilus* is a poem about the failure of a love which seemed for a time, at least to its hero, sublime, and with this point the fact that Troilus and Criseide are not married has nothing to do, except insofar as it enhances the intensity of the erotic experience—a potentiality that has always been known, in all ages, to all poets. Despite its dealing with unmarried love, the poem is as highly moral as its author, and in the best sense; and I might point out that the word *moral* and its derivatives are almost wholly unexampled in English until they erupt in Chaucer's works, including *Troilus*. By stressing a phantom cult of sexual immorality in the Middle Ages, literary historians distract the reader from what is really morally significant in some of the greatest medieval writers. It was perhaps inevitable that the great burgeoning of interest in courtly, immoral love should have occurred at a time when sexual morality was once more threatening (the phenomenon seems recurrent) to replace all other forms of morality—in the late nineteenth and twentieth centuries.

I conclude that at least a part of what is called courtly love was no more real in the Middle Ages than it had been before and has been since. As far as the better part is concerned, which I have been calling sublimation, that was surely real in the Middle Ages, and since then has acquired the added reality of becoming a myth. It may be that things are now changing, though I feel that even the modern anti-novel is a back-handed tribute to the durability of sublimation. And it seems to me that there is little about the conventional assumptions of medieval love literature that an intelligent and mature reader will fail to apprehend without special briefing; what was really new and significant in medieval love has become part of our inherited response to existence.[1]

---

[1] The number of works consulted for information and opinion is too large to be listed; those I have used or abused most directly are as follows: Andreas Capellanus, *De Amore Libri Tres*, ed. E. Trojel (Copenhagen, 1892); same, *The Art of Courtly Love*, tr. J. J. Parry (New York, 1941); J. F. Benton, *Speculum*, xxxvi (1961); A. J. Denomy, *Speculum*, xxviii (1953); W. T. H. Jackson, *RR*, xlix (1958); Amy Kelly, *Eleanor of Aquitaine* . . . (Cambridge, Mass., 1950); C. S. Lewis, *The Allegory of Love* (London, 1936); Gervase Mathew in *Essays Presented to Charles Williams*, ed. Dorothy Sayers *et al.* (London, 1947); Gaston Paris, *Romania*, xii (1883); D. W. Robertson, Jr., *MP*, l (1953); same, *A Preface to Chaucer* (Princeton, 1962); F. N. Robinson, ed. cit.; and the *Oxford English Dictionary*. My colleague Professor Elizabeth S. Donno has recently pointed out to me that Sir John Davies in his poem 'Orchestra' (1594) uses the phrase *courtly love* thrice (stanzas 5 and 50); but his sense seems less the modern one than that of *OED*, *courtly*, 3, 'elegant, refined', or 4, 'characterized by the fair words or flattery of courtiers'.

12

MEDIEVAL POETRY AND MEDIEVAL SIN

IN RECENT YEARS scholars have shown a steadily increasing interest in the problem of sin in medieval literature, so that nowadays it is a rare issue of a journal devoted to the Middle Ages that does not contain an analysis of the sin or sins committed by Gawain, or Chauntecleer, or Beowulf, or Troilus, or the Nightingale, or even the Wife of Bath. It seems widely accepted that in order properly to understand medieval fiction one must get its personages exactly placed on the sin-spectrum—if possible, to the nearest millimicron of pride or lust. This business of hamartiametrics is admirably moral, and since we all recognize that the Middle Ages were profoundly Christian and that sin is an important if negative element in Christianity, it would appear to be a legitimate function of criticism to assess the medieval version of human behaviour from a sin-oriented point of view. With this in mind, I recently went through the Chaucer *Concordance* with the purpose of making an analysis of all Chaucer's uses of the word *sin* as well as of the words for the individual members of the deadly septet.

What I derived from this labour was, critically speaking, disappointing: pages and pages of statistical material proving only the simple point—which I suppose should have been obvious to me in the first place—that words for sin occur mostly in sinless contexts: that is, where sin is being talked about rather than practised. For instance, while the word *sin* itself (noun and verb) occurs in the *Canterbury Tales* 467 times[1] (and only twenty-one

---

[1] The items in the *Concordance* counted (at the rate of ten to the inch) were *sin* noun, verb), *sins, sinneth, sinned, sinning*. In addition, *sinner* occurs 4X Pars ; 1X Mel.

times outside the *Canterbury Tales*),[1] all but seven of the Canterbury occurrences are in moral tales, sermons, or strictly neutral contexts. The Parson's Tale alone, which is, of course, all about sin, accounts for 416 uses, 85 per cent of the Chaucerian total and 89 per cent of the Canterbury total, while another 44 uses are scattered among the Man of Law, the Physician, the Monk, the pilgrim Chaucer,[2] and others who speak in behalf of virtue. Thus the pittance of seven is thinly spread over those writings in which the density of genuine sin is highest, such as the Miller's, Reeve's, and Merchant's Tales and the Wife of Bath's Prologue.[3] In general the same kind of proportion holds for the names of the specific sins, which are also far commoner in the mouths of the righteous than of offenders. I was furthermore disappointed by the fact that the most promising of the few uses of *sin* in sinful contexts—as by January and the Wife of Bath—have been thoroughly discussed by previous workers in the field, who have, indeed, left few stones unturned in their search for the worm of sin.

There remains, however, one occurrence of the word in a context of extreme misbehaviour which has not, to my knowledge, been fully considered, and I should like to take up this usage here in the hope that it may throw some light on the problem of sin in medieval English poetry. The word *sin* does occur—just once—in the Miller's Tale. When Nicholas is instructing John the carpenter about the arrangements that must be made in order that the *ménage à trois* may survive the Second Flood he emphasizes that while he and John and Alison are in their suspended containers, up under the roof, they must not speak with one another, but occupy themselves with prayer: for, he explains, that 'is Goddes owene heeste dere'.[4] He then goes on to warn the carpenter that he and his wife Alison must hang far apart so that between them there 'shal be no sinne—Namore in looking than ther shal in deede'.[5] Now John seems at once to accept the validity of this prohibition without questioning its

---

[1] The non-Canterbury count is 7X *Bo*; 6X *TC*; 3X *LGW*; 2X *ABC*; 1X *Anel*; 1X *FormA*; 1X *RR* (Frag A).

[2] 17X *Mel*; 7X Pard; 4X ML; 4X Phys; 3X WBT; 2X Mk; 2X SN; 1X Sum; 1X Mcp; 1X GenPro (narrator); 1X MilPro (Reeve); 1X ClPro (Host).

[3] 1X Mil; 2X WBPro; 4X Mch.

[4] A3588.   [5] A3589–90.

authority, and perhaps, if I were tactful, I would too: but critics hot on the trail of sin cannot afford to be tactful, and hence I propose to try to fill in the doctrinal background that might seem to lie behind Nicholas's prohibition, with the hope of better understanding why John accepts so unhesitatingly.

Before beginning the investigation, let me claim the privilege open to all medieval analysts of sin, or analysts of medieval sin, and make several rather fine distinctions—rather fine and, I must confess, quite arbitrary: if we eschewed arbitrariness we analysts might find our analyses fatally diminished. And so in my reading of the text I have persuaded myself that when Nicholas issues his prohibition he is not claiming it to be a rule made *ad hoc* by the Almighty for this single occasion: that is, it is not a part of his account of *Goddes owene heeste dere*. Furthermore, I reject the argument that John would have recognized this particular Monday night as a time of penance, a time in which sexual intercourse between married persons was, of course, forbidden—though I allow some merit to the opinion that it would be becoming to the chosen survivors of another deluge to show some voluntary restraint before the event, especially since the first time the Lord bent His bow against the earth the cause was man's lechery. Finally, I do not think it likely that a day of general inundation would be properly considered as a Holy Day or High Feast, when John would have been aware that intercourse was forbidden. No, I suppose that none of these possibilities would have weighed very heavily with John, and that the reason he did not question Nicholas's injunction was that he found it perfectly natural, inasmuch as he had probably been given reason to assume that every time he lay with Alison or even looked at her with lust in his eye (apparently it was difficult to look at her in any other way), he was guilty of sin.

In order to test this theory, it seems reasonable to look up late fourteenth-century doctrine about marital intercourse in the kind of manual of sins that John's parish priest in Oxford would have been acquainted with. To the reader of Chaucer such a manual lies ready to hand in the Parson's Tale; and in order to reconstruct the proper medieval context, one might put oneself in the position of a parish priest interpreting to John the Parson's strictures. Actually, this is not very easy to do, for the Parson's remarks on marital intercourse are not entirely coherent, and they offer as well certain problems in what might be called human engineering. His first observation is that, since one must love God more than any earthly thing, a man must not love his wife excessively.[1] This basic tenet concerning loving God would probably be comprehensible even to a man as untutored as John, though it might flash through his mind that as a matter of practical expediency a discussion of marriage is not the happiest context in which to be reminded of it. Even a more sophisticated husband than John might sincerely assure his God that he loves Him more than any earthly thing, but be reluctant to inform his wife that he loves her, as the Parson says he should, discreetly, patiently, and temperately:[2] few wives would appreciate such moderation. I think at this point it might be borne in on John that the Parson was not a married man, so that his strictures were untarnished by experience. This would certainly occur to him when he heard the Parson's account of the reasons for which man and wife may have sexual union. There are three of these:[3] the first is for procreation; the second is in order that each spouse should render to the other his bodily debt; the third is to avoid lechery; and the fourth is deadly sin. As for the first, procreation, it is meritorious; so too, though less unabashedly,[4] is the second, payment of debt; the third, forestalling of lechery, is venial sin—and here the Parson casts a long shadow backward when he adds that 'truly, scarcely may there any of these be without venial sin, for the corruption and for the delight'. And the fourth of these three reasons for which a man and wife may assemble is solely for amorous love, which is mortal sin.

If John were my pupil, I am afraid that I should find it hard to make clear to him the difference between payment of debt (a function that seems to embarrass many of the orthodox

[1] Parson's Tale, 1.1855. Marriage is, of course, considered under the heading *Luxuria*.
[2] 1860: 'Man sholde loven his wif by discrecion, paciently and atemprely'.
[3] 1935–40.
[4] The only example the Parson gives of meritorious conduct in the payment of debt is that of a wife who 'hath merite of chastitee that yeldeth to hir housbounde the dette of hir body, ye, though it be again hir liking and the lust of hir herte' (I 940). What the husband's status is the Parson fails to make clear.

authorities into murkiness,[1] so that it is most clearly defined
by the Wife of Bath) and the avoidance of lechery; or how, in
the (apparently unlikely) event that the two spouses love one
another, it is possible to keep amorous love from getting into the
act of paying debt or of preventing lechery. I think the best
thing to do with John would be to avoid further definition and
follow the Parson in placing emphasis on the special virtue of
joylessness, assessing, as the Parson effectively does, the amount
of sin involved in the act as approximately equalling the amount
of pleasure derived from it. John could then go home and try
to puzzle out for himself where he stood in regard to sin.

If John had lived in Kent, he might have received instructions
somewhat less dampening than the Parson's from a priest
trained by the manual of Dan Michael of Northgate. Michael,
following his relatively liberal source Friar Lorens, considers
both spouses unequivocally meritorious when they are rendering one another their debt.[2] He even allows merit to the motive
of avoiding lechery, though under a rather special circumstance:
that is, when a wife is so modest that she cannot bring herself to
ask her husband to satisfy her and is thus in danger of falling
into lechery—presumably with another man—it is meritorious
of the husband to forestall her.[3] John might, I think, take comfort from the second part of this proposition, for it is clear that
Alison is constantly in danger of falling into lechery. It is true
that one does not get the impression that this danger is caused
by an excess of modesty in Alison, but then I must confess that
I find it a little hard to imagine the woman Dan Michael has in
mind: Pope's catalogue of female self-contradictions includes
women who die of nothing but a rage to live, but the paradox
of one driven to *luxuria* by shamefastness seems to have eluded
even Pope. Still, the tenor of Dan Michael's definition seems

[1] See last note. In general, the more austere authorities seem to feel that St Paul
went regrettably far when he enjoined spouses to render to one another their
debitum (I Cor. vii, 3). The King James translators circumvented the embarrassment
by rendering the word as 'due benevolence' like other translators before them.

[2] *Dan Michel's Ayenbite of Inwyt, Or, Remorse of Conscience,* ed. Richard Morris
(London: EETS OS 23, 1866), p. 222.

[3] Ibid.: 'Þe þridde cas is huanne me hit acseþ his wyue of þo dede uor to loki
hire uram zenne, nameliche huanne he yziȝþ þet hi is zuo ssamuest þet hi nolde
neuremo acsi hare lhorde of zuiche þinnge, and ylefþ þet hi ssolde ualle bleþeliche
into zenne oþer liȝtliche bote yef me hire ne acsede.'

more liberal than the Parson's, and this is true also of his consideration of the sin of purely amorous love. While for the
Parson this is invariably mortal, for Dan Michael it may be
either mortal or venial. That is—assuming that my Middle
Kentish is adequate—if a man afflicted with lechery controls
it so well that he would not perform the sexual act with any
one but his wife, then his sin is venial; but if, on the other hand,
he is so lecherous in his love for his wife that he would perform
the sexual act with her even if she were not his wife, then he is in
deadly sin.[1] I say that this distinction possesses some liberality,
but I must confess that it possesses more liberality than clarity,
and I doubt that John, wedded to Alison, would understand its
logic, or theologic, if only because I don't understand it myself.
Indeed, I could hardly blame John if at this point he were to
turn away muttering,

> 'Ye, blessed be alway a lewed man
> That nought but only his bileve can.' (A3455-6)

I should be most happy if in instructing John in the niceties of
marital sin I could use as my authority neither Michael nor the
Parson, but Robert Manning of Bourn. Robert's source, William
of Waddington, had refused to go into what he called certain
privities of sin, and I'm sure that his genial adaptor enthusiastic-
ally welcomed this tactful decision.[2] The result is that intercourse between married persons is a potential sin hardly handled
in Robert's *Handling Sin*. All he has to say on the subject is that
man and wife should not lie together at times proscribed by the
Church—what Langland calls *untime*—and these are easily defined for the simplest intelligence.[3] Aside from that, Robert
speaks only of a sin that one supposes the average couple would
find fairly easy to avoid: married persons should not have

---

[1] p. 223: '[Me may zeneʒi liʒtliche] huanne þe lost ne paseþ naʒt þe markes ne þe
zetnesses of spoushod. Þet is to zigge huanne þe lost is zuo yled mid scele þet þe
ilke þet is ine þet stat nolde naʒt þet þing do bote ine his wyue. Ac huanne þe
lecherie and þe lost is zuo grat ine his wyue þet scele is yblent and ase moche wolde
do he ine hire þaʒ hy nere naʒt his wyf, ine þet cas is þe ilke zenne dyadlich'.
[2] *Robert of Brunne's 'Handlyng Synne'*, ed. F. J. Furnivall (London: EETS OS 119,
123, 1901-3), lines 30-4 (English), 83-4 (French); 8407-11 (English) and parallel French.
[3] Lines 2008-14, 2021-4 (English); cf. *Piers Plowman*, B IX.186.

intercourse in church or churchyard; for, Robert says, if they do so *custumably*, it is deadly sin.[1]

It seems to me that the difference between the approach represented by Robert and the one represented by Michael and the Parson is that Robert, despite the title of his book, is much more interested in sinners than he is in sin, while the other two are so engrossed by sin that they have no energy left with which to learn and care about the creatures who commit it. It is as if they had taken the old precept, 'Hate the sin, not the sinner', and misinterpreted it as an injunction to define the sin with complete exactitude without paying any attention to the human requirements of the sinner. They apparently don't worry that their definition is either so rarefied as to be beyond the comprehension of people of normal experience or else so all-inclusive as to deprive sin of any positive value. Dan Michael's constructs of the woman turned whore through modesty and of the man turned whoremonger through uxoriousness are examples of the former, and the Parson's yoking of delight with corruption in married love is an example of the latter. Both men are celibate thinkers: in the case of Dan Michael this results in an inability even to start thinking about married life except through an enormous effort of the imagination, by which he is propelled to a platform in space where no law of gravity acts to impede his mental acrobatics or to draw him down to the realities of earth. In the case of the Parson, the effect is subtler: he is in the ancient tradition of thinking of marriage exclusively in terms of a husband who really would have preferred to be a celibate but somehow in his youth made the rash mistake of taking a wife whom he now deplores, regarding her partly as a peril to his spiritual state, partly as just a nuisance (incidentally, insofar as the Parson allows us to see the wife's point of view, she seems understandably unexhilarated by her husband). The curious thing is that in its general tone the Parson's attitude toward marriage reminds one of nothing so much as the attitude of January in the Merchant's Tale: while wholly in disagreement on the potential sinfulness of marital intercourse, the two are remarkably alike in regarding the wife as at best a vaguely animate object in a marriage, not as a partner in it, so that one

[1] Lines 2015–20 (English).

could not say with confidence that it was January's view of marriage that produced the Parson's rather than the Parson's that produced January's. Both think of a wife not as a woman but as a tun, or a bit of veal, or a knife sheathed or unsheathed through matrimony.[1]

To revert to the simple carpenter of the Miller's Tale, I think it safe to assume that we would have lost him in our discussion of sin some time ago. He seems on the whole to have been a respectful man, and a pious one, and I suppose that he would feel he ought to give as much weight to his priest's incomprehensible instructions on marital love as he did to nightspells addressed to the White Pater Noster and St Peter's sister, and that he would come away from the lesson feeling properly guilty. Yet I rather doubt that he had the leisure in which to brood over the implications of his guilt. After all, he was a very hardworking carpenter, one who sometimes worked over the whole weekend procuring timber for the local monastery. Add to this the inevitable emotional exhaustion that would result from his having to guard Alison so carefully and you do not have the picture of a man with much time or energy available to worry about the lecherous aspects of his love for his wife. One even wonders how much opportunity he had to practise his lechery. Alison seems to have been a skittish creature with a mind of her own, and one suspects that John sometimes found himself sinning in looking when he would have preferred to be sinning in deed. Of course the sin is known to be just as deadly, though it is certainly not as satisfactory to the sinner, and I doubt very much that a man suffering from frustration from an inability to sin in deed has the energy to worry over the fact that he is now sinning in his will. My conclusion, therefore, is that John naturally accepted Nicholas's injunction (with which I began this investigation) that even to look at Alison on the night of the flood would be sinful, but that in general he failed to bother himself much about his marital lust because life was just too full. Or, in other words, as an old man wedded to a young wife, he was too busy paying for his sin against nature (perhaps his

---

[1] The Parson uses the images of wife as knife (with which a man may slay himself) and as tun (from which a man may get drunk) at 1855-60. January uses the knife image (denying the Parson's sense) at E1838-40; for the veal image, see E1420.

only genuine sin) to think of himself in the Parson's terms. Probably the Parson's attitude was to him academic; and possibly the academic was to him, as to many people, something one both respects and, for reasons of time and space, disregards.

Obviously there is a world of difference between John the carpenter and his creator Chaucer. Yet both were busy men, both married, both makers—of ladders or lecherous lays, kimnels or couplets, by whose aid they hoped to weather the storms of life, including married life. And I am inclined to think that to the poet as well as to the carpenter the niceties of sin— and not only the niceties, but the very fact of sin—may have sometimes seemed academic when he was not operating directly under the Parson's influence. It is true that at the end of the Parson's Tale Chaucer expresses remorse that he has not always operated under such influence; but this hardly seems an excuse for doing what so many scholars have been doing lately—trying to undo the effect of Chaucer's retraction by making it appear that the spirit of the Parson's Tale actually informs all the works for which Chaucer specifically apologizes. It seems to me wrong to read, as so many wish to do, the Parson's Tale as a reliable gloss on the rest of the Canterbury Tales, for to many of the tales sin is simply not relevant. Theologically we may all be in a state of sin or in a state of virtue, but that is not the only guise under which a poet may wish to consider us. For not every poet is a Dante, wholly preoccupied with whither our lives have tended and performing God's work by assigning us residence—within his text—in hell, purgatory, or heaven. A poet who wishes to speak of us as we are on earth will take our sinfulness for granted and go on from there to matters which, for the moment, interest him more. Virtually all the great lovers of literature are, of course, either fornicators or adulterers, but the poets who created them are in general far less interested in that fact than they are in the human love whose value, one way or another, the lovers enhance; and even Chaucer for once peeps into the hereafter to suggest that that notable fornicator Troilus was awarded a better life there than he had while being lustful here. To say that Troilus was motivated by lust—as the Parson would—is a statement which to the poet must be at once supremely obvious and wholly inappropriate.

It is similarly inappropriate to observe that the Miller's Tale is a tale about lechery. Heaven knows there is a good deal of lechery in the air, and no one could argue that the characters are leading a kind of life that would receive St Cecilia's seal of approval; but the Miller's Tale is not about lechery, it is about a world that contains much lechery, but also, and more important, contains gaiety and high spirits and large folly and great wit and a marvellously naughty resourcefulness of the imagination. I'll agree that all the characters are now in whatever hell is reserved for characters who misbehave in fiction; but I hope that it is a hell designed by the best medieval imaginations, one with really witty devils and only the most fantastically ingenious of torments—one, in short, designed by Chaucer, and thereby a hell unique in being blessed by his unfailing sense of what is apropos.

The Parson's Tale seems a most inappropriate gloss for many of Chaucer's best poetic writings. It may be unexceptionable in its theological doctrine, but in literary terms it is ill-tempered, bad-mannered, pedantic, and joyless, and when it is used as a gloss to the other tales it distempers them, fills them with ill humour, coats them with dust, and deprives them of joy. I suspect that to reduce everything to the Parson's orthodox technicalities is to miss the point of poetry. Surely it would be more sensible and humane to use the rest of the tales as a gloss on the Parson's, counteracting its morbid negatives with a few of their healthy affirmatives. After all, what Chaucer was good at was not the formulation of doctrine on sin but the revelation of the marvellous variety of life in a world which, however sinful, is the only world we've got, and one that can mingle much delight with its inevitable corruption. The best medieval literature does not necessarily have anything to do with sin, and it does just what Chaucer does—offers joy to the reader. And that, despite the Parson, is no sin.

To go back once more to John and his putative sin, I must say that I am in a way sorry that he was not instructed by a relatively liberal teacher like Robert Manning—or, for that matter, by William Langland. If he had married young, John's youth would have been comforted by Langland's most succinct comment on marital intercourse, though as a *senex amans* he might have found it less cheering:

> ... Whil thou art young and yeep, and thy wepne keene,
> Awreke thee therwith on wiving, for Goddes werk ich holde it.
>
> (c XI.287–8)

On the other hand, as I have suggested, it is doubtful that any outside authorities would have much affected John's love for Alison, damned though this may have made him by Church and by nature. In this connection, one cannot help thinking of that expert in marital misdemeanour, the Wife of Bath, looking back on her life with her extraordinary ability to comprehend her own and the world's complexity: accepting as fact that what she most liked to do was sinful, aware though not much troubled that her soul was imperilled by her having so often done what she liked, but still regretful that because it was sinful she had been unable to do it more:

> 'Allas, allas, that evere love was sinne!' (D614)

Thus she puts the whole matter into a nutshell, for herself and, I think, for many poets of all eras.

INDEX OF PROPER NAMES

This index lists references to scholars, to literary and historical personages, to titles of literary works whose authors are unknown, and to Chaucer's works and the fictional characters in them. Not included are the editors of Chaucer mentioned only on page 120, note 2, or Chaucer's works mentioned only on page 165, notes 1 and 2.